MORE PRAISE F

Addicted to Stress

"*Addicted to Stress* offers women a wise and insightful way to recognize their patterns of stress, how this damages their daily existence, and the necessary strategies to improve their lives. By guiding us toward self-recognition and honesty, Debbie Mandel advises women to refocus their goals and behaviors in order to achieve rewards and satisfaction."

—Susan Shapiro Barash, author, *Little White Lies,*
Deep Dark Secrets: The Truth about Why Women Lie

"Debbie Mandel has distilled years of experience in helping so many people in this inspirational and useful guide to living a more joyful and full life. Pearls of wisdom fill every chapter. This book is a must-read for everyone who desires better coping skills for stress and anxiety—and take your time!"

—Dr. Mark Liponis, corporate medical director,
Canyon Ranch

"Debbie really hits the nail on the head. I think most of us women suffer from some stress addiction at various points in our lives, and Debbie gives great advice on how to respect and take care of yourself! It's a must-read for all women!"

—Chris Freytag, fitness expert, *Prevention Magazine,*
and author, *Short Cuts to Big Weight Loss*

"This book is an excellent guide for all women like me who don't feel human unless they are pressured. *Addicted to Stress* not only helps us recognize our addiction, but also guides us step-by-step to overcome the effect of this condition and restore balance in our everyday lives. This book should be a mandatory read for every woman entering the workforce and raising a family. I will recommend it in my health care practice."

—Ellen W. Cutler, D.C., author, *Live Free from*
Asthma and Allergies

Addicted
to Stress

Addicted to Stress

A Woman's 7-Step Program to Reclaim Joy and Spontaneity in Life

Debbie Mandel

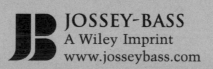

JOSSEY-BASS
A Wiley Imprint
www.josseybass.com

Copyright © 2008, 2010 by Debbie Mandel. All rights reserved.

Published by Jossey-Bass
A Wiley Imprint
989 Market Street, San Francisco, CA 94103-1741—www.josseybass.com

No part of this publication may be reproduced, stored in a retrieval system, or transmitted in any form or by any means, electronic, mechanical, photocopying, recording, scanning, or otherwise, except as permitted under Section 107 or 108 of the 1976 United States Copyright Act, without either the prior written permission of the publisher, or authorization through payment of the appropriate per-copy fee to the Copyright Clearance Center, Inc., 222 Rosewood Drive, Danvers, MA 01923, 978-750-8400, fax 978-646-8600, or on the Web at www.copyright.com. Requests to the publisher for permission should be addressed to the Permissions Department, John Wiley & Sons, Inc., 111 River Street, Hoboken, NJ 07030, 201-748-6011, fax 201-748-6008, or online at www.wiley.com/go/permissions.

Readers should be aware that Internet Web sites offered as citations and/or sources for further information may have changed or disappeared between the time this was written and when it is read.

Limit of Liability/Disclaimer of Warranty: While the publisher and author have used their best efforts in preparing this book, they make no representations or warranties with respect to the accuracy or completeness of the contents of this book and specifically disclaim any implied warranties of merchantability or fitness for a particular purpose. No warranty may be created or extended by sales representatives or written sales materials. The advice and strategies contained herein may not be suitable for your situation. You should consult with a professional where appropriate. Neither the publisher nor author shall be liable for any loss of profit or any other commercial damages, including but not limited to special, incidental, consequential, or other damages.
The anecdotes in this book are based on the life experience, work, and research of the author. To protect confidentiality, some of the names and identifying characteristics have been changed or represent composite identities.

Jossey-Bass books and products are available through most bookstores. To contact Jossey-Bass directly call our Customer Care Department within the U.S. at 800-956-7739, outside the U.S. at 317-572-3986, or fax 317-572-4002.

Jossey-Bass also publishes its books in a variety of electronic formats. Some content that appears in print may not be available in electronic books.

Library of Congress Cataloging-in-Publication Data
Mandel, Debbie Eisenstadt.
  Addicted to stress : a woman's 7-step program to reclaim joy and spontaneity in life / Debbie Mandel. — 1st ed.
      p. cm.
  Includes bibliographical references and index.
  ISBN 978-0-470-34375-3 (cloth)
  ISBN 978-0-470-48590-3 (paper)
  1. Stress management for women. I. Title.
  RA785.M355 2008
  616.9'80082—dc22   2008020974

Printed in the United States of America
FIRST EDITION
PB Printing 10 9 8 7 6 5 4 3 2 1

CONTENTS

To my loving family both on earth and in heaven
And to my husband, Steve, "Baby, You're the Greatest"

PREFACE

I was about to sit down on a cushioned lawn swing, cup of coffee in hand, and inhale the beauty of my garden. But then I surveyed a few imperfections, a mottled leaf here and a dangling flower there. Oh, look at that awful weed invading my perennial bed! I let my coffee get cold while I set to work pinching and clipping, the envy of any worker bee.

Suddenly, I heard a mocking voice inside my head: "A woman's work is never done."

Why did this old line pop into my head? Strange—I couldn't recall ever having read it.

Then I laughed as it hit me. The crows squawked too as a great white heron flapped his wings. Here I was about to sit down and relax, take a few moments of quiet time in a serene setting; but no, I found a few things to do, as though nature needed me to improve her art and I needed to perform so that others could say, "Wow, look what Debbie did!"

Stress had invaded my safe haven, my garden. I went into the house and Googled the old familiar saying. I found "A Woman's Work Is Never Done," written in 1795 by Martha Ballard, stanza after stanza depicting the tedious schedule of an eighteenth-century woman.

■ ■ ■

There's never a day, from morn to night,
But I with work am tired quite;
For when the game with me is at the best,
I hardly in a day take one hour's rest;
Sometimes I knit, and sometimes I spin,
Sometimes I wash, and sometimes I do wring.
Sometimes I sit, and sew by myself alone,
And thus a woman's work is never done.

■ ■ ■

This was the "aha" moment when the concept of *Addicted to Stress* was born in my head. The words of thousands of women who attended my classes, workshops, and interactive Web site sang out the modern-day refrain:

"I have to rush."

"I'm crazy busy."

"I've got a million things to do."

"I don't know when I will get everything done."

"I can't remember what it feels like to get a good night's sleep."

Instead of living happily ever after, women everywhere are forever on high alert, forever responsible, and forever giving. The worst part of this is that women—my students, my colleagues, myself included—all seem to be trapped in a terrible habit of continuing, never-ending, self-driven activities that are in response to what we perceive to be terrible pressures at home and, for many of us, in the workplace. We can't stop, we're addicted to stress, we're stress addicts!

I wrote this book to liberate us: the endless to-do list must end! We can't keep missing the simple truths in life while trying to be so perfect, clever, and accomplished.

Stress addiction is equivalent to *identity theft*—and we are the thief robbing ourselves of joy and spontaneity. Many of us don't know who we are anymore, let alone know the dreams of the free-spirited girl living inside us, the girl we were before we became the good girl, somebody's wife, mother, colleague, and friend.

You must stop being that good girl. In this book, I'll show you how to turn stress into strength, to cure your addiction as you build up an immunity to outside pressure and learn how to be your true core self again.

Join me and many other women who are overcoming their addiction to stress. And after you read this book, I hope you'll ignite your inner light and let it shine brightly.

Acknowledgments

A special thank-you to my editor, Alan Rinzler, for his eloquent, sequential thinking, which kept pace with my associative mind. What a great wit! He has made me shine.

Thank you to my literary agent, Andrea Hurst, who loved the book and my "Debisms" and took me by the hand to guide me in formulating a winning proposal. Andrea is not only a wonderful writer in her own right but also a warm, nurturing person in a competitive world.

Thank you to Frank Mikulka, who continues to teach me all about fitness. A former Marine, he is an elite and creative trainer and martial artist, popular for his warrior classes for men and women.

Thank you to Nana Twumasi, Carol Hartland, Jennifer Wenzel, Jeff Puda, Paul Foster, and Debra Hunter, all from Jossey-Bass/John Wiley & Sons.

Thank you to my children, Michael, David, Amanda, and daughter-in-law, Lisi, for putting up with me when I talked about the book—constantly—and for eating some of my overcooked dinners when I lost track of time writing the pages.

Thank you to my dear and loving husband, Steve, who has to deal with my feistiness and outrageous sense of humor—does he have a choice?

Addicted to Stress

STEP 1

Be Aware of Your Own Stress Addiction

The first step in our process of change is to understand ourselves, to accept the fact that yes, we have a problem. But never fear, there's definitely something we can do about it.

My research with thousands of women has taught me that the biggest universal problem women have today is our attitude toward stress, the daily dynamic tension of our lives. In fact, I've learned that living with stress for women these days has become more than a habit: it's an addiction.

That's right. Addiction. Just as with drugs or alcohol. Stress has become so ubiquitous (a fancy word for common, widespread, pervasive) that we're used to it, we expect it, we're actually uncomfortable if we don't have it.

Sisters (and some brothers), listen up. We've reached the point where we've got a "jones" for stress. It has taken over our lives like the extra thirty pounds or unwanted guest at the dining room table who refuses to leave.

Addicted to stress.

How did this happen, and what can we do about it?

Taking a Hard Look at Ourselves

Women today carry massive responsibilities of family, household, and career. It often feels to us as if we're being blown about in so many different directions that we're battered into exhaustion.

Ironically, we call this progress. We need to ask ourselves two questions:

Are we satisfied?
Are we happier?

Well, certainly men are happier. Two studies from Princeton University and the University of Pennsylvania indicate that a happiness shift has occurred over the years. In the 1970s, women used to be *slightly happier* than men; now men have exchanged places with women. The reason for this change is that men have cut back on unpleasant activities and now relax more, spending quality time with the family. Research shows that meanwhile, women have been taking on more complex tasks than they did four decades ago. They have replaced housework with paid work, but that doesn't mean that the work at home has disappeared. Women's to-do lists have grown; the number of waking hours to get everything done has not.

When tasks don't get crossed off the list, women experience stress resulting in sleepless nights and days filled with feelings of negativity and inadequacy. The studies emphasize that because women now have opportunities for accomplishment on many new levels, they tend to believe that if they don't "do it all" the home, the marriage, the job—they don't measure up!

The Impact of Too Much Stress

Bottom line: if you are unhappy with yourself, then all your relationships, including your most intimate, will be filled with unhappiness. And further research from Sigal Barsade of the University of Pennsylvania explains that bad moods are contagious. Your family will absorb and mimic your behavior, thereby perpetuating a negative loop.

Although the medical community has established that a little stress is actually good for you—waking up your creativity, fueling your vitality, and keeping your immune system vigilant—the qualifying and key word here is *little*. When you find yourself rushing from activity to activity, doing chore after chore, with no personal time for yourself, the problem isn't the external world that's landing on your doorstep; rather, it's your own need to constantly open that door and welcome stress into your life!

Why We Love Stress

Most likely you are addicted to stress because of the adrenaline rush—the "look what I can do" syndrome. You're so productive! You do it all, get it all—mother, wife, worker, with boundless energy 24/7.

However, having plenty of physical energy should not be confused with vital, focused energy. The critical question you must ask is, How do you distinguish a stress addict from a healthy high-energy person? And here's the answer: the physical energy of a stress addict is always moving forward, living in the future, accomplishing the next task on the addict's to-do list, or worrying about what will happen later, rather than experiencing reality in the present. In contrast, a high-energy person intensifies her present to experience it fully.

What It's Like to Be an Addict

You might think that the term *addict* is a harsh word for simply being busy. But it is the right word. You may say that the conventional perception of an addict is of someone so focused on her bad habits that she is a very selfish person, whereas so much of a woman's time is dedicated to being unselfish, to taking care of her family. But let's look at the fundamentals of addiction, and we'll see why *addict* is the right term.

Common to all unacknowledged addicts is the illusion that they have some sort of power and can control their behavior. However, when we take a closer look, we can readily see that this is a totally false perception; addicts are in fact without self-awareness and have little or no control over their compulsive activities. For example, a gambler thinks she can control her luck, an alcoholic her drinking, and a pot addict her smoking. However, an unaware addict cannot tap into her personal power. To numb the pain, the feelings of worthlessness both overt and subtle, a stress addict hides herself in the great escape of distraction.

The fix of busyness leading to apparent accomplishment gives the stress addict a kind of high that sends pleasure signals to the brain. But, as is true of all addictions, the high is transitory. The addict needs another high and then another, the ever-expanding to-do list, to sustain that false euphoria.

Admit it. Oh, how you love the surge of adrenaline energy as you rush to perform your activities and duties! You feel important.

TALES OF STRESS ADDICTION
Do They Have Adult Cliffs Notes?

Sara had found no time to read the book she had suggested for her book club members. She was agitated about tonight's opening remarks, beating herself up about it. Should she fake it or admit that she didn't read the book and let someone else run the meeting? Perhaps she should not attend the meeting and say she is sick! Sara tried to read the four hundred pages, but couldn't concentrate or get into the book. She felt as if she were back at school and unprepared for a test.

I asked Sara why she had joined a book club in the first place if she is not a reader and is busy with her work and the children. She quickly explained, "For the social benefits. I like to get together with the girls once a month and talk." I suggested that she attend the session and throw out an opening question based on the book jacket, allowing others to run with it. She could join in with examples from life experience, movies, or other books. Fun should not be stressful. Evaluate your clubs and activities. Are you overbooked?

You feel powerful. After all, you are a very busy person. During your high, you are always venturing outward, escaping; therefore, you don't have to go inward, to return to your own doorstep—the components, problems, conflicts, and deficits of your real personality, or at least what you think it is.

So you can't be still or alone. Deep down, you fear your own quiet company the most.

Are Addicts Bad People?

No. Emphatically not. Addicts are not bad people. Addictive behavior is basically a survival mechanism to deal with what is perceived as an unhappy reality.

Addicts are good people. You could argue that highly successful people are just working hard in our normal workaholic workplace culture. I've learned, however, that in the case of stress addiction, all this busyness usually stems from the addict's constant need to prove herself. Are you suppressing feelings of unattractiveness, unworthiness, and inadequacy that are nevertheless seeping out through the seams of your body and soul?

A Self-Test for Addiction Awareness

How can you tell that you are a stress addict and not merely a busy person who is responsible and reliable? Answer the following questions:

1. Do you tune out during conversations? (For example: Do you scan the top of your friend's head while you barely listen to the conversation, thinking about other things?)

    ___ Yes ___ No

2. Do you feel rushed wherever you are because you feel that you ought to be completing the next task somewhere else?

    ___ Yes ___ No

3. Are you irritable with others?   ___ Yes ___ No

4. Do you rate yourself according to the opinions of those with whom you interact? Do you seek a "Wow" as a response for what you do? ___ Yes ___ No

5. Are you unable to ask for help? ___ Yes ___ No

6. Do you perceive being on the *receiving end* as a sign of weakness? ___ Yes ___ No

7. When you exercise, do you do it for longer than sixty minutes, five days a week? ___ Yes ___ No

8. Are you always talking on your cell phone—even when taking a walk? ___ Yes ___ No

9. Do you constantly check your appearance in the mirror? ___ Yes ___ No

10. Do you feel uncomfortable, worried, nervous in your mind or body when you don't have something you must absolutely do right now? ___ Yes ___ No

If you answered yes to

3 questions: You are out of balance.

5 questions: You are losing your sense of self.

10 questions: You have hit the crash-and-burn zone.

The purpose of this questionnaire is to help you pause and notice.

Profile of a Female Stress Addict

As a woman, you experience stress with greater intensity than a man does, as you process words and body language more quickly using both sides of the brain (which predisposes you to multi-tasking) and have a deeper limbic system, the seat of emotions (which connects you more sensitively to all your relationships). Consequently, you are more prone to depression and often respond with emotional outbursts, which can be particularly awkward at the workplace.

When this emotional intensity is regularly activated by the various kinds of stress you experience, you become even more vulnerable to sadness and irritability. Stress becomes generalized as you experience a free-floating uneasiness and lose the capacity for calmer, more positive solutions. As a stress addict, you adhere to the same pattern of the "over-doer" at home, at work, and in all your relationships. Guess what? There is no such thing as a separation of work and home—though you'll see well-intentioned efforts in pop culture to label the work-life balance—because you are the same person on Sunday night as on Monday morning. The balance or imbalance rests with you. As a stress junkie, you bring a common perception to all the major categories of your life:

Without you, nothing works.

Stress challenges our equilibrium, unsettling us, and our response to it ranges from mild to intense. Sometimes stress is

TALES OF STRESS ADDICTION

Back to School

Mary is breathing shallowly, speaking quickly, and acting defensive about her son's first semester at college. "We're finishing the first term. We can't believe how difficult those two humanities classes are. My son is a business major. Why does he need Writing the Essay and Western Civilization classes? I'm having trouble keeping up with all that reading and writing."

Clearly the umbilical cord has not been cut. All this vicarious pressure must be stressing out Mary's son, Jeremy, as well. Mary needs to concentrate on her own work and find some creative hobbies.

recognizably nerve racking; at other times it is more subtle and vague, even hidden. Can you recognize it in your own life? Let's take a closer look at how stress can manifest itself in the three compartments of your life.

At Home

- You do not delegate chores or allow others to contribute—it's your way or no way.

- You hover over your children as a helicopter mom.

- You are much too cheerful with your spouse and children, who may actually be annoyed by your cheerfulness.

- You are impatient, easily angered.

- You feel anxious and pressured about the clubs for which you have volunteered, such as the PTA, the American Association of University Women, or the neighborhood book club.

- Sex is one more thing on the to-do list (maybe).

- You experience sugar lust or a craving for fatty comfort foods.

- You don't sleep well.

At Work

- You bring work home with you and take your BlackBerry on vacation.

- You brag to the boss about how little sleep you got the previous night.

- You are not really a team player; you horde your work or are secretive with colleagues who might steal your thunder.

TALES OF STRESS ADDICTION

Mind-Reading Gone Awry

Carol and Lainie, who work for a software company, were assigned a prominent market research project to evaluate the competition for the company's new software product. During the first week of the project, Carol kept seeing Lainie working on other assignments, and she was seething. Finally she lashed out at Lainie for not pulling her weight. Fortunately, Lainie calmly explained that she was tying up loose ends, clearing her desk, so that she could devote her complete attention to their project. Carol's mind-reading almost sabotaged the team spirit. I explained to Carol that work is all about integrating one's personal rhythm with others'. She needs to be aware of her personal triggers and stay on the alert to being tempted to cross the line into negative mind-reading.

- Colleagues annoy you. They talk and laugh too loudly while you are working.

- You focus on the one colleague who doesn't greet you or doesn't like you, even though most of your coworkers are sociable and friendly.

- You worry about your family (your aging mother, your children's SATs) during work.

- You eat lunch at your desk and need a donut and coffee during the afternoon slump.

- You feel unappreciated; you want to quit but won't; you have a love-hate relationship with your job.

In Relationships

- You expect your spouse and friends to read your mind, to know what you mean even when it's evident that they can't figure out where you're coming from or what you want.

- You get caught up in repetitive, purposeless arguing.

- You have trouble receiving a gift: "Oh, you shouldn't have . . ."

- You are hungry for compliments. You want to be thought of as attractive, but don't think you really are. You are competitive with your girlfriends.

- You are sensitive to criticism.

- You view all your relationships in terms of accomplishments.

The Value of Awareness

Changing your life profile for the better requires that you gain an honest awareness that something is amiss, sapping your positive energy. The first step involves observing your behavior. You need a little distance to see the whole picture, the way you observe a friend and then give that friend some good advice. Only this time, you will show some compassion for yourself, befriend yourself, and take your own advice!

The secret to any success is having the determination to succeed, then taking small, patient steps, evaluating and tweaking them along the way without any pressure. Step 1 of this program is all about becoming aware, in a nonjudgmental way, leading you to determine *what* is wrong, not *who* is wrong. You are simply noticing.

The motivation to improve will become part of your mindset when you start to truly see. When you complete this program, you will compare how you used to experience a glitch, a remark, or a schedule change and how you experience it now—with an easy smile. So, gently lift the curtain and take a peek at the full-blown symptoms of stress addiction. Could this possibly be you?

Symptoms of a Stress Addict

Here are more symptoms to watch out for. The ones listed earlier addressed behavior; these are on a more internal level:

The loose mind. The most telltale sign of a stress addict is a *loose mind*. You do all your chores and social activities with a kind of porous consciousness, unfocused on the here and now. You lose your mental boundaries, unable to exclude extraneous thoughts. You are the consummate multitasker. Even on your child's school trip for which you volunteered, or on a visit with your mother, or at a ball game with your husband, you are speaking on your cell phone most of the time, communicating with the workplace, home, friends, the plumber, the physical therapist. You are kidding yourself believing that you are really spending quality time with your loved ones. Although it might seem paradoxical, you would accomplish more through *single-minded tasking*—tightening your mind—but you do not believe this. Instead, your loose mind causes you to waste energy, feel tired, and grow irritable.

The dramatic vocabulary. Think about the words you use daily. "I'm crazy busy." Words define your reality and have a way of actualizing a prophecy. When your friend bemoans her hectic day, you brag about yours: "Oh, you think *you're* busy, listen to this . . ." If life were calmer and filled with free time, you probably would not know what to do with yourself. You might not want to sit still and be with yourself because there are pockets of

Tips for Curing Stress Addiction
Experiencing Technological Karma

Most of us know The Feeling of not receiving our e-mail for a few hours because our e-mail provider's server is down. You are cut off from a fast-paced world, and there is nothing you can do about it. After the initial frenzy during which you actually think you have some semblance of control over the situation, you settle into an "It's out of my hands" mind-set. Then you start feeling more relaxed, disconnected from the stress of 24/7 technology for a while. You have more time—found time—for yourself.

I experienced this compulsory hiatus for two weeks during an already hectic media tour. Irritated that my e-mail provider wasn't even taking my phone calls, imagining that the company was going out of business, I decided to adopt a wait-and-see attitude and just let it be. A couple of weeks later, normality returned, and guess what? I was surprised to learn that I hadn't missed much. The "universe" was trying to tell me something. Now I take voluntary breaks and no longer fear that I am missing out. I am actually finding more within.

disappointment and unfulfilled dreams you don't want to contemplate. For if you did, you would have to do something, make a move, risk failure and rejection. It is easier to distract yourself by speeding things up and at the same time making yourself indispensable to others. Or so you think.

The great performer. Stress addiction is driven by the constant need to prove your self-worth, to show that you are a valuable person. You reap the reward for being the consummate go-to person. In fact, your voracious appetite for compliments motivates you to hunt for them constantly to feed your ego. Because you have built your reputation around the title of the "doer," what will be left to distinguish you from other successful women?

Delegate work? No way—then you would not get to shine as superwoman. The problem is that *you can no longer separate who you are from what you do*. If you fail at a task, you feel like a failure as a person because your tasks define you. You are usually anxious, whether you are presenting in the board room or addressing the League of Women Voters. What will people say about your performance?

The guilty sinner. Stress addicts always feel guilty about having fun and relaxing. You might say, "I'm so happy, I can't stand it!" There is an internal conflict between what you want to do and what you think you ought to do. And if you *are* enjoying yourself, you feel as if you are tempting fate; you think of the blissful heroine in a typical soap opera, heaped with adversity the moment she proclaims she has never been happier. It's as though fear will protect you from a bad thing, and happiness predisposes you to disaster. In other words, being overwhelmed with work is your insurance policy against tragedy.

The sacrificial giver. Giving is your signature specialty and makes you feel good about yourself. When you receive a gift, though, you follow it up with, "Oh, you shouldn't have." Imagine how the bright, smiling face (of your daughter, husband, fellow worker) droops when you invalidate a gift.

Let's be honest. You are the consummate people pleaser. Please preface your name with "Saint." However, your eagerness to be the giver and to do for others depletes your energy reserve and positivism. Internally, you feel resentful and are running on very little gas. You are out of balance, about to tip over with all this giving! Also, you have actually made others second class, always coming to you for help.

The inattentive listener. Often you go through the motions of being present to others. But while you are speaking on the phone, you might be checking your e-mail, cleaning out a drawer, exercising on a treadmill, driving the car, and so on. You don't think listening attentively is a good enough reason to cease all other activities. This is a self-imposed adult version of attention deficit disorder. You don't have a genetic or biochemical problem with how your brain works; rather, you *choose* not to focus your attention. Don't think, however, that the other person doesn't know or sense that you are not totally present. There is a subtle pause in your voice; you respond to a previous question a little too late, or you do not follow the conversation completely and are a little confused because you have missed some of the sequential details. Sometimes you are engaged in a face-to-face conversation, and this is trickier than over the phone, where you can believe that the other person can't see that you are multitasking; face-to-face, your eyes betray you. Whereas a natural and attentive conversationalist focuses on the speaker's eyes and literally bathes his face with listening cues, the stress addict looks elsewhere, eyes scanning for more action. Your subtle message to the speaker is, "You are not worth my total attention. I am extremely busy, an important person who carries the world on her shoulders and can only squeeze you into my day while I think about the next task on my list."

The great controller. You have grown more irritable because you are disappointed that people and situations do not act according to your requirements. You feel that other people must behave in sync with your expectations and within your time frame. Speeding through life makes patience a nonstarter virtue. For example, you have a doctor's appointment scheduled for your son. The doctor keeps you waiting forty-five minutes. You look at your watch every couple of minutes. You go up to the sign-in sheet and check where the list is going and if anyone has been called ahead of you. When your child's name is finally called, you wait with him in an examining room for another fifteen minutes. By this time you are crazy and forget half the questions you wanted to ask the doctor (unless they're on your to-do list, which is now ten pages long). If only you could let go of your "must" requirement, you could utilize the time more efficiently, such as by nurturing your child.

The stern inner critic. Stress addicts are not only critical of other people but also highly critical of themselves. You wonder, Am I thin enough? Am I accomplishing enough? Do I have the lifestyle I expect and deserve? One of the telltale signs of stress addiction is that you compare yourself to the most attractive, happy, or successful person in the room, never focusing on your own unique attributes and accomplishments, never content with yourself. A negative coach lies at the root of your personality, whipping you on: *You are not good enough!* Past accomplishments do not satisfy your inner critic—they are over and done with. It's as though your good qualities don't register with you.

Hooked on pain. Exercise addiction mirrors stress addiction. If you want to see a stress addict in action and understand what she is experiencing, go to an all-night gym. Exercise addicts carry the expression "no pain, no gain" to the max. If they don't hurt physically or feel exhausted—annihilated, so to speak—they keep on exercising. I have heard comments like these in the gym: "That was an amazing class. I could barely breathe. I call it death by step!" "What a great training session—he killed me!" Instead of engaging in a health-promoting exercise program (no more than sixty minutes of exercise), the exercise addict erodes the joints, damages internal organs, and triggers depression with *combat* fatigue. Exercise addicts are highly critical of their bodies and never feel thin or attractive enough. They pound their bodies into submission to achieve a semblance of control. However, their workout rules their life as they organize their day around the exercise session.

Numb from the waist down. For the stress addict, sex becomes another performance-driven obligation. The media implies that you need to be capable of being aroused at a moment's notice as well as choreographing an amazing athletic love work-out. And don't forget to be multiorgasmic in the process. How-ever, if you're a stress addict, making love makes you yawn. Stress has depleted your vitality. You would rather sleep. At the heart of the matter, you are avoiding intimacy with yourself! You don't eagerly slide into pleasure because you don't view sex as an ac-complishment, and besides, there is no one there to validate your performance, except for your spouse, who doesn't count. It is also difficult to perform well in the bedroom when your self-image is not at an all-time high. Your stern inner critic is always nagging, and your body might be changing because of childbirth and the natural aging process.

Understanding Why

Now that you are taking a closer look at your life, you might be wondering how you got suckered into this kind of maddening, heart-deadening lifestyle. If you are to manage your stressors, you need to understand the general root causes. Here are some pos-sible reasons that might resonate for you.

Toxic Feedback from the Past

Did your parents compliment you only when you achieved aca-demically or athletically? Were you a bit sensitive to criticism because of bad experiences at school with teachers who graded you rigorously and classmates who hurt your feelings by making fun of you, adding insult to the injury of high parental demands?

If the answer to either of these questions is yes, make every effort to escape getting stuck in the past. Just become cognizant of your current adrenaline-charged lifestyle. You are no longer a child needing validation, a "Good girl!" Nor do you have to fol-low tribal beliefs that don't make any sense to you—even if they come from your parents or your community.

TALES OF STRESS ADDICTION

Cleaning Out Your Closet

Realize that it is easier to be incredibly busy than to deal with layers of grief accumulated during the course of a lifetime. Dealing with emotional issues from the past is like cleaning out a messy closet—who wants to clean out a closet? You would rather be hectic with other chores where your performance can be validated and applauded. However, cleaning out a closet is a private matter and involves letting go of what no longer serves you, so that you can see more clearly what you need and really use. And chances are that if one closet is filled with clutter, there are many others, along with drawers, and there might even be a basement or attic! However, when you clean out just one closet, the rest is much easier to do, as you are motivated by the initial successful results. Similarly, tackle any one of the layers of mental clutter, and you get at the source, because they all share the same theme—that's why you don't have to keep digging into past resentments ad infinitum. Keep your thoughts relevant to what you are doing today instead of confused with the past, to ease up on yourself, in a small and simple way, so that the process feels more like cleaning out your pocketbook instead of a whole closet.

Whenever I clean out my pocketbook, I feel a great emotional release. I might not even understand what kind of junk I have cleared out of my head while I was deciding what to throw away or keep, but I feel better. The point is that I come away from the task having created more room to see what remains inside, the special things I have forgotten about amid all the clutter, and so will you.

Don't overwhelm yourself in frenetic activity, even for a noble cause. How can you ease up on yourself today—in a small and simple way? What is really stopping you from doing less and letting go? In the case of curing stress addiction, less is more. Gandhi said, "There is more to life than increasing its speed."

The Sandwich Generation Is Growing Stale

Being sandwiched between aging parents and developing children can disguise a stress addict as an altruist, for after all, caregiving is a noble endeavor. "What would you have me do? Abandon these helpless individuals?"

For example, Nili, one of my clients, is the consummate caregiver. She is taking care of two teenage boys along with her first-grade daughter and helping her widowed mother recover in Nili's home from a hysterectomy that had unforeseen complications. Because it is *her* mother, she tiptoes around her husband, Jack, who isn't crazy about her mother living with them even for a few weeks.

Nili typifies the stressed-out performance addict. She martyrs herself for everyone else because deep down she doesn't believe

---

 Tips for Curing Stress Addiction
Your Paycheck and Housework Stress

Did you know that in married working couples, the more money a woman earns, the less housework she will do? So says sociologist Sanjiv Gupta of the University of Massachusetts at Amherst. That finding is based on a study of women who work full-time. The critical element, Gupta explains, is how much money the woman makes, not how much she makes compared to her spouse. If she earns $40,000 or more, she's going to spend less time doing housework than a woman who earns less. In other words, shedding or delegating chores is directly tied to a woman's subjective quantifiable sense of her own self-worth and is not linked to her position relative to her husband. Is how much money you make your mirror—the ultimate definition of your self-worth, giving you permission to relax and fulfill yourself? Consider this: no one can pay you what you are really worth.

that she has accomplished enough and earned the right to be happy. She can't cut the umbilical cord that nourishes all the members of her family. She is also the household generator; everyone's plugged in to her energy socket. There is no need to investigate Nili's childhood or look into her tribal beliefs to find a conditioned pattern of selflessness and perfectionism. The world is not conspiring against her; the obstacles are internally driven! Romance is no longer enticing to a depleted woman. How can she possibly feel sexy? Jack is getting tired of her saying no to him.

The Biology of Stress 101

Admitting the truth is an important step in the recovery of any addiction. However, what truly seals the deal is realizing what stress does to you, how it inflames your body, mind, and spirit. Is it worth it to be sick and tired, or out of focus?

When you respond to a family member or coworker with anger due to stress, you may feel hyperalert because of the adrenaline rush (the hormones adrenaline, norepinephrine, and cortisol rushing throughout your body); however, in reality you are using the most primitive, reptilian part of your brain, the fight-or-flight inner core. You will probably say things you later regret, send that e-mail you wish you had never written, or beat yourself up with "I should have said . . ." What you should be using instead is the most highly evolved part of your neurological system, the cerebellum and neocortex at the top front of the brain. To do so means consciously observing that you are stressed and taking a break to relax.

Ultimately, stress robs you of an optimistic resiliency that allows you to adapt to various obstacles; instead, you're hitting your head against a wall in frustration.

If you only knew what stress does to your body, you would stop stress in its tracks!

TALES OF STRESS ADDICTION

Hitting a Wall Hurts

Michelle called me up in tears. After hearing her story, I sent her directly to the emergency room and then met with her the next day. Raising two preschoolers as a single mom and feeling conflicted about her new promotion in the marketing department (more pay, but more responsibilities), Michelle felt inundated. Getting both the children and herself out the door during the morning rush was tense, especially when the kids were fooling around. She would scream and insult them, then feel guilty for losing it with a three-year-old and a five-year-old. This particular morning, while screaming at her children, she walked smack into her metal front door and broke her nose badly!

Michelle realized that being upset caused her to be unaware of her surroundings. We came up with some concrete morning strategies to ease the tension, such as preparing the children's clothes and lunches the night before and waking up fifteen minutes earlier. After her surgery, there was compulsory rest from work; during the healing time, Michelle decided that all this agitation wasn't worth it. She could see the pattern and stop it.

Stress and Body Chemistry

Here's what happens when you experience stress. Powerful hormones are released throughout the body, elevating blood pressure and putting the senses on high alert. Glucose is driven up to the brain and into the muscles. Your evolutionary preprogrammed response is fight or flight. However, in modern times whom do you fight—where is that proverbial saber-toothed tiger? Of course, it's your spouse, family members, friends, and colleagues. How do you interact with others when you feel stressed?

Do you put on boxing gloves, arguing tit for tat, or do you flee from the room and slam the door shut—the home version of the fight-or-flight response?

Do you know that you live with powerful stressors night and day? Consequently, powerful stress hormones are continuously flowing throughout your body, inflaming organs, metabolic processes, and emotions, and making nerve endings raw. That's why stress needs to be systematically released, because it is toxic to health and happiness. If you are going green, concerned with shedding processed foods in your diet or chemicals in your home environment, then you need to be equally conscious about shedding toxic emotions like anger and resentment. Stress causes you to fall into negative perception, subtly at first, without your awareness. Only now you will know the reason.

Four Modern-Day Stressors

The four stressors that bombard our bodies daily and simultaneously are environmental, physical, internal, and national.

1. Environmental stress consists of air, land, and water pollution; radiation; food additives; pesticides; cleansers; and chemicals.
2. Physical stress includes bacteria and viruses in our bodies, allergies, aches, aging, and injury.
3. Internal stress is self-induced stress: unrealistic expectations, grief, living in ambiguity, feeling helpless or hopeless, and experiencing relationship woes.
4. Our national vulnerability to terrorism induces fear and anxiety.

Stress is enmeshed in our lives, leading to fatigue, insomnia, overeating or loss of appetite, poor concentration, excessive worry, allergies, frequent colds, and aches and pains. A generalized negativity infiltrates the spirit, making you feel sad and disempowered and causing your creativity to decline.

Tips for Curing Stress Addiction
Stress Is the Tipping Point for Disease

Scientists at the University of Saskatchewan's Vaccine and Infectious Disease Organization have uncovered that signs of stress in proteins and other compounds found in the blood can help predict susceptibility to disease. It's well known that exposure to viruses or bacteria causes disease in some individuals but not in others. This study helps clarify how the stress level of an individual affects the infection process and the severity of disease. During seasonal outbreaks of viruses and bacteria, like the flu, make sure to include daily stress management as a part of your health regimen. When you wash your hands, wash away your negative mind-set.

Identify Your Personal Physical Stress Response

Note how your body reacts to stress to understand how to create your individual relaxation response. Your choice for relaxation might involve physical or social activity, using humor, visualizing, meditating, or creating your own synergistic combination based on your unique needs. Throughout this book you will learn specific relaxation response cues, even the various foods to eat, to release your specific type of stress.

1. You may feel a variety of emotions: anxious, angry, tense, resentful, irritable, fatigued, or depressed. Each of us has a personal emotional "stress profile." What is yours? When you identify your stress profile, you can direct specific strategies to promote relaxation.

2. It's useful to pay attention to the body parts that commonly become afflicted when you are feeling stress: head, jaw, neck, shoulders, stomach, back, joints, and skin.

3. You may either get the munchies or lose your appetite.

Tips for Curing Stress Addiction
The Biophysical Response

Listen to what your body is trying to tell you—metaphorically.

Here are some physical cues that can help you decode your stressful mind-set. When your neck hurts, are you unyielding in an argument? If you have a headache, are you overanalyzing? Do your shoulders hurt because you are shouldering too much responsibility? Does your back hurt because you feel unsupported? If your skin itches, what are you itching to do? Do you have acne because you are erupting in anger? Does your stomach hurt because your ego has been undermined? Do you get diarrhea because you need to get the crap out of your life? Do you have a urinary tract infection because someone is pissing you off?

Your body serves as a metaphor for what is happening in your mind. Think about where it hurts and how that might relate to the root cause of your problem. Your inflammatory physiological discomforts in turn provoke inflammatory language, setting you on fire with anger or causing burnout. You get caught in an inflammatory loop. However, the opposite is also true. You possess the power to put out the fire. You can change your negative perception to forgive, release, or laugh, moving on to a yet more positive perception. Challenge your anger with a rational explanation. Realize that stress is causing you to lose perspective. Listen to what your body is trying to tell you. The next time you are losing it and don't know why, let that painful weakest link in your body provide the clue to letting go of the disturbing mind-set.

4. You may experience sleep disturbances, either in falling asleep or staying asleep.

5. Your breathing can become shallow and more rapid.

6. Some people experience dizziness.

7. Whereas some people feel hyperalert, others cannot concentrate and are easily distracted.

Your body is trying to tell you something. Take note, because sometimes you have to leave your overly analytical, locked-in-worry mind to get into your senses to experience pleasure.

Two Kinds of Stress: Acute and Chronic

Stress management involves quickly recognizing stress responses, both covert and overt, to stop them before they do damage. First, be aware that there are two types of stress, acute and chronic. Not all stress is bad, and that's a great relief, because who can live a stress-free life? Acute stress heightens the senses, enabling you to live in the moment.

Acute stress can help you take action when you receive bad news or a bad diagnosis. For example, if you accept a diagnosis with total passivity and inertia, you might not go for a necessary second opinion or attend a support group. When you become an active partner in your own health, you channel normal anxiety into positive energy.

In contrast, chronic stress is damaging. The latest research from Harvard, for example, shows that caregivers face a 20 percent higher risk of mortality than the rest of the population because of the daily stressors they face.

The Type D Personality

According to the American Medical Association, a new personality type has been identified as one more prone to inflammation, particularly heart disease and stroke, than the Type A (which

Tips for Curing Stress Addiction
The Glass Half Filled

Try this exercise to let go of overload and the resentment that accompanies it. Hold a glass half-filled with water. It feels comfortable in your hand. Keep holding it. Your hand is starting to ache. Hold it for half an hour, an hour. The glass gets unbelievably heavy, and your hand hurts terribly. Now put the glass down. What a relief! Pick it up again and hold it for a few minutes. Put it down.

The glass represents your overloaded life and the inevitable resentment it brings. Who can carry even the smallest resentment for long without feeling overwhelmed by the pain, without having it take over one's whole consciousness?

Put the glass down and feel relieved. You can always pick it up again if you want to for a few moments. Do yourself a favor, though, and put it down.

pales in comparison): the Type D personality, distressed and distant. The Type D has trouble tolerating her own imperfections and perceives asking for help as a personal shortcoming; both attitudes are barriers to intimacy.

For a Type D, change can be overwhelming because the unknown invites fearful visions. Consider this: you can walk a plank on the ground with confidence, remaining on the plank without slipping off to the ground. Now elevate that same plank ten feet, and you are frightened that you will lose your balance and fall. It is not your body that fails you, but your *mind*, which conjures up failure. The Type D personality is terribly afraid of living her life: What will people say? What if she should fail?

Use It or Lose It!

Even when you feel distressed about having lost all control—because of the aging process, for example—you can exert the mind, your powerful control center. Observe how some older people look young and act young even when chronologically advanced in age. Some people who get cancer feel alienated from humanity; others come to their senses. Make up your mind to live with enthusiasm, experiencing one focused action after another. Obviously, no one is going to live forever, but you can really be happy while you are alive. Choose not to listen to your self-doubts by redirecting your thoughts toward what you love doing, toward relaxation. You are not stuck, because you *can release your physical and mental overload.* Choose to put the half-full glass down and create your own calm center.

Whereas our prehistoric ancestors experienced tangible physical threats that triggered life-and-death stress responses, we usually face emotional threats, such as being ignored at a party, feeling embarrassed when making a speech, or getting criticized at work. Your thoughts control your body. That's why the placebo effect works. Before you even learn how to beat stress and lift your mood, start by minimizing small daily stressors, such as by releasing some of your duties and asking for help. You might not be able to tackle the huge chronic stressors just yet. However, by reducing your stress overload with small, manageable changes, you will reap giant gains immediately.

Keep in mind: the stress response during prehistoric times was adaptive behavior for survival. However, now that survival is easier, stress comes at a great expense to your health and happiness because there is no tangible outlet. The point is that you have to make a concerted effort using both mind and body to release stress. Awareness is a necessary first step in cultivating a relaxation response. In the following chapters you will learn concrete

Tips for Curing Stress Addiction
The Four Rooms Exercise

In the **physical room,** you eat healthy meals and snacks; eat a rainbow array of fruits and vegetables; drink plenty of water; take a power hour to do your own thing; exercise daily, whether by walking, lifting weights, or dancing around the house; get enough sleep; and organize your day around good health. In the **emotional room,** you establish boundaries, express your true feelings naturally, ask for what you need, delegate chores, and come to your senses instead of numbing them. In the **intellectual room,** you learn from reading, watching movies, and listening to others. Some chance encounter might transform your life for the better. Three words from the woman ringing up your order at the supermarket can be your breakthrough moment. In the **spiritual room,** you activate your compassion; don't just talk about it. This might mean volunteering once a week at your community center, letting someone with a couple of items precede you at the supermarket, holding the door open for an elderly person, or giving a sad stranger a warm smile.

When you address your physical, emotional, intellectual, and spiritual stressors by walking into the four rooms of your home, your immune system becomes vigilant; thinking clears and energy soars. If a problem should arise, you will deal with it. Instead of falling into a negative worry loop, you can take the necessary steps to solve your problem, asking for help when you need it and evaluating your success along the way, flexible enough to try plan B or plan C. If you observe yourself slipping while under pressure, take note of your physical stress-response cues and interpret them to reestablish balance quickly. Your body will let you know if you are successful; this is your own form of biofeedback.

coping tools that will build confidence in your ability to cope with the stress of modern day living as you experience greater well-being. You are building up a resistance to feeling bad, the same way you might get your immunizations and booster shots.

Step 2, Reclaim Your Identity, will help you achieve *homeostasis*, which in terms of stress management means balanced physical and emotional well-being, in order to treat yourself as an individual whom you hold in high esteem. Liberating yourself from stress addiction means identifying your true self and the inner message that can propel you forward to a happier life. It's time to reveal who you really are and identify your real purpose in life.

■ ■ ■

Are you ready to reveal your hidden dreams, take stock of your unique gifts, and reclaim your identity? An original like you does not need to settle for living a contracted life without meaning! Your personality quest in Step 2 will lead you on a journey to embrace yourself and reclaim your joy and natural self-expression. It's high time you answered these questions: Where do I fit and with whom? And do I even need to fit?

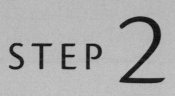

STEP 2

Reclaim Your Identity

The second step to eliminating the stress in your life involves turning your focus inward and getting reacquainted with who you were before you became a wife, mother, and caregiver.

Getting reacquainted with this former self is like picking up where you left off with an old friend with whom you've lost touch over the years. It's like reviving that hidden girl who still lives so gorgeously within you, that blithe spirit, the unfettered, playful, thoughtful, sweet and sensitive, madcap, playful, lusty, kinetic, blushing, funny, high-spirited, hair-down, top-drawer, secret flamer. The real you.

TALES OF STRESS ADDICTION

Molly's Forgotten Identity

Molly was visiting her mother at the nursing home. Although in the middle stages of Alzheimer's, her mother still knew Molly, for which Molly was grateful. One day, her mother smiled at Molly, recognizing her as someone familiar, but unable to recall the specific relationship. "So I started singing to her like I did when I was a little girl. And she knew all the words and started singing too. So we both began singing together at the top of our lungs like two lunatics, then we laughed and laughed. We created quite a stir in the day room. Sure, my mother didn't know what was going on, but she started to feel who I was, and she was having such a great time, fully alive and in the moment. My hidden girl came out full tilt and joined with her in that affirming moment as best we could under the circumstances. Something in both of us was liberated."

Each of us has our own unique hidden girl within. You can remember her, right? She has survived these stress-filled years in spite of being suppressed. The real you is still there! A cautionary word: don't return to the past seeking to release an innocent, inexperienced girl. You are no longer a child. It's time to get back in touch with your natural self—without all the masks you wear for others.

As a woman, you are hardwired to be relationship oriented and flexible—perhaps too flexible. In fact, you tend to bend over backwards. Now it's time to stretch and reach out to become more flexible concerning your own needs. Because you are inherently creative and strong internally, it's time to give birth to yourself again! Know that your own rebirth will infuse your family with new, life-giving energy because you are the true center of the household.

Therefore, in the midst of being crazy with busyness, stop for a moment and ask yourself: What happened to that hidden girl within?

Have you been the victim of identity theft?

Stress Can Steal Your True Identity

The most far-reaching negative consequence of stress addiction is *identity theft*. By this I mean that stress steals your capacity to be your natural self and instead creates an artificial you, a woman who can't sit still and spend quiet time alone or do something special just for yourself, but instead must always be doing something, doing more and more, for everyone else!

The result is that you feel not only exhausted but also impatient, indecisive, and disempowered—constantly fearing the imminent potential of concluding your day underaccomplished!

Meanwhile, you've lost your real self and are too tired to search. "What does it matter anyway?" you may say. "I have to take care of all these people."

Apparently it matters a great deal, because there's someone out there running around with your *personality debit card*, withdrawing from all your accounts, stealing all your time and energy. You can't catch up with her to see who is masquerading with your name. You can't stop her from this abusive behavior. She's ruining your credit rating.

The Journey Inward

To start the process of reviving that hidden girl within and reclaiming your real identity, you must accept two stipulations.

■ ■ ■

1. You were born an original. You don't need to become a shadow of your former self or a copy of someone else's concept, merely because you live and work with others. Stop acting second-rate. Don't rate yourself according to what others say about you. Instead be first-rate, taking the initiative to fulfill your true self.

2. You must create time for introspection. You might be reluctant to do so. You might associate introspection with adjectives like *oppressive*, *painful*, and *depleting*; maybe you think introspection leads only to "Okay, now what do I do with all this misery?" However, the introspection I have in mind for you is a fun and liberating pathway to exploring your secret inner joy.

Metamorphosis Made Easy

Butterflies are an ancient, universal symbol of transformation. Normally, we don't consider an egg, caterpillar, or pupa to be beautiful. It's the dazzling butterfly that lures our attention. On a butterfly farm in Costa Rica, I experienced the magic of metamorphosis close up, where I realized that each stage of life has its

Tips for Curing Stress Addiction
Your Daily Power Hour

For you to rebalance your daily life, you need to keep the pendulum swinging freely in both directions. Schedule pleasurable time and space on your daily to-do list. An hour is a suggested, doable period of time. If this is too much time for you to allot for personal pleasure, try a smaller block of time—thirty minutes, fifteen minutes, even five minutes. Who doesn't have five minutes? Whatever motivates you to slow down and experience positive energy must be given high priority in your life. This special time will revitalize you, enabling you to perform everything else more effectively. When you see how good you feel, you will find ways to increase this time.

own beauty. I saw pupae that looked like golden earrings and miniature Fabergé eggs. Contained in each stage is a mysterious energy and beauty that wants to fly free. So, like a butterfly, allow yourself to be overtaken by the natural process of transformation, accepting that change happens in stages. Shed what no longer serves you, and emerge into your true, natural self that does not suppress its colors and engages in synergistic relationships, not toxic ones.

Do, however, get rid of the butterflies in your stomach when you feel stressed. They don't belong in there, trapped in negativity. Release them into the light.

Just Breathe

When you were born, the first thing you did on your own to exert your separate identity and announce your presence to the world was to breathe. Breathing immediately became routine, and throughout the years you probably haven't given it much thought.

Tips for Curing Stress Addiction
Questions to Help Revive the Hidden Girl Within

- What makes me happy?
- What do I enjoy doing when I lose track of time?
- What energizes me rather than depletes me?
- What helps me serve myself in order to serve others?
- What do I need to clearly communicate, so that others understand what I need?

As your stress levels soar, your breathing becomes more shallow and quick. To be on a first-name basis with your real self, you need to return to your breath. Breathe naturally, inhaling and exhaling. While you are breathing to your own natural rhythm, think, "With each breath, I now relax my heart." Focus on your heart. Feel your breaths getting deeper and your blood pressure going down. Repeat this rhythmic breathing for ten breaths. Now you feel relaxed, as you grow more aware of your personal rhythm.

Harness Your Power

Identity is tied to seeing yourself as separate from others in the context of all your relationships. How do you differ from your spouse, family members, and friends? Through contrast you can see yourself as distinct, better able to define yourself. Distinction leads to self-appreciation.

Don't worry about seeking constant applause for a job well done; do things with integrity just for yourself, even when no one is looking. Think of the fine art cabinet maker who completes the back of a wooden chest with polish and detailed carving even though the chest will be placed against a wall where no one will see that part of it. You need to get into the habit of pleasing yourself more and to develop the courage to be unavailable to those who steal your time. Base your availability to others on your energy level. Say no to the energy vampires in your life.

A Shortcut to Identity

The search for identity need not be the result of a crisis. It can resemble a treasure hunt with ideas and images popping into your head as in a word association game. Here's a quick, easy personality test to help you get started on unveiling your hidden girl within.

Answer the following four questions briefly; don't agonize over them for hours, just let your heart speak spontaneously, without inhibition.

1. What is your favorite color and why?

2. What is your favorite animal and why? (It doesn't have to be a pet.)

3. You're in a narrow room with windows, but no electric lighting. The room is getting cooler; twilight arrives, and the room becomes darker. Suddenly you see a little opening in the wall, and a beam of light shines through the aperture. How do you feel when you see the light?

4. What is your favorite body of water and why? (This could be something in nature, a bottle of Poland Springs, or a shower.)

 Tips for Curing Stress Addiction
How to Breathe Deeply

Many of my clients tell me that using only the nose for breathing—inhaling and exhaling along with a visual cue—creates deeper breaths and therefore a greater relaxation response. So try this . . . Sit or lie down. Close your eyes. Breathe by inhaling two long counts through the nose and exhaling four long counts through the nose. When you inhale, imagine inhaling a white mist, clean and fresh. As you exhale, imagine releasing a dark mist of used-up old stuff.

Here are some sample answers and what they meant to specific women who have attended my workshops and trainings. They may not be exactly true for you, but they do reveal how this test can work for many individuals. For more details, please refer to my Web site, www.addictedtostress.com, where you can e-mail me if you get responses that you can't interpret.

■ ■ ■

1.   What is your favorite color and why?

SAMPLE ANSWER	WHAT IT MEANT TO ONE WOMAN
Red because it is bold and energetic	I am bold and energetic.
Yellow because it is fun	I have a fun-loving personality.
Blue because it is serene	I am a calm person.
Green because it is healing and nurturing	I am a soothing caregiver. I am Dr. Mom.
Purple because it is royal	I want to be respected.
Brown because it is earthy	I am real and down-to-earth.
Orange because it is bright	I am cheerful and optimistic.
Black because it makes me look thinner	I like to be mysterious.
White because it is crisp and fresh	I am proper, always appropriate, and well groomed.
Pink because it is sweet and feminine	I embrace my femininity.
Gold because it is rich	I appreciate financial achievement and invest wisely.
Silver because it gives me a special glow	People gravitate to my power.
Off-white because it is creamy and looks good with my skin	I know how to show myself off to get results and am comfortable with my appearance.

2. What is your favorite animal and why?

SAMPLE ANSWER	WHAT IT MEANT TO ONE WOMAN
Hawk because it is free and powerful	I am a free spirit.
Wolf because it is independent, yet part of the pack	I have a unique voice in a team effort.
Kitten because it is warm and cuddly	I am an affectionate person, highly expressive.
German shepherd because it is intelligent	I am a sharp person, mentally alert.
Cockatiel because it is chirpy and flies	I value freedom and adventure, like to come home when I want to.
Butterfly because it is so colorful and fragile	I am beautiful on the outside, and when that fades, I am beautiful on the inside.
Seal because it is so playful	I love to play and know how to release my inner child.
Dolphin because it is a friendly sea mammal	I am highly social, functioning well in different groups.
Tigers because they are formidable and protect their family	I am a protector and potential stalker who knows how to get what she wants.
Dog because it is loyal and loving	I am a loyal and affectionate person.
Fish in my aquarium because they are graceful	I am graceful and flexible, and can swim in many environments.
Horses because they are fast, sleek, and strong	I am strong and fast in the direction I decide to take.
Lions because they rule the jungle	I want to be on top of the pyramid and set the course for others.
My teddy bear because it is soft, cuddly, and low maintenance	I am affectionate and easy to please.
Swan because it is beautiful and graceful, and mates for life	I know my worth and am loyal.
Monkeys because they are fun and mischievous	I am playful and love to laugh. I have a naughty side.
Rabbit because it is cuddly and gentle	I am gentle and maternal.

3.   How do you feel when you see the light?

Remember that the cues were *narrow room, getting cooler, becoming darker,* and *beam of light coming through the wall.* This is how you feel about closure, endings, life stages, moving on, or graduation. Closure can mean the end of one life stage before the beginning of another, such as being single and then getting married. Ending some stage of your life need not be frightening, as it is often accompanied by positive change and rebirth.

SAMPLE ANSWER	WHAT IT MEANT TO ONE WOMAN
Curious	I would rather know the truth than pretend.
Relieved	I tend to fear the worst, but am usually relieved by what actually happens.
Eager to see the light	I am spiritual and believe in the greater good.
Frightened	I am afraid of the dark and ambiguous. I need proof.
Serene	I stay calm in the face of adversity because I am accepting.
Agitated	I don't know how I feel because I am ambivalent.
Confused	Sometimes I believe optimistically about things and other times I second-guess myself.
Lonely	I like to travel with a companion, especially to unknown places.
Emotional	My powerful feelings have been awakened, but I don't have a name for them.
Insecure	I am not sure if I will measure up.
Summoned	I know I have a mission—but what is it?
Enlightened	I am eager to understand everything.
Alien	I am suspicious of new places, jobs, parties. Sometimes I feel alienated.
Grateful	I appreciate my past experiences, have learned from them, and do not look back with regret.
Inexplicable happiness	I have a great, open heart.
Mystical	I have an ability to see deeply into ordinary things.

4.   What is your favorite body of water and why?

Psychological studies have shown that water symbolically expresses your feelings about sex. Traditionally water symbolizes a woman, just as a tower or other phallic image symbolizes a man.

SAMPLE ANSWER	WHAT IT MEANT TO ONE WOMAN
A **bath** because it is relaxing.	I am comfortable with my body.
The **deep sea** because I love scuba diving.	I am not inhibited about exploring my partner and likewise being explored.
The **ocean** because it is rhythmic and powerful.	I am in rhythm with my partner and feel waves of delight.
A **waterfall** because it is refreshing.	I feel energized.
A **lake** because I love to dip my feet in.	I am cautious and proceed slowly.
I **can't swim** and feel more comfortable on land.	I am a bit fearful of making myself vulnerable to another person, unable to control the experience.
Puddles in the rain because they remind me of childhood fun and experimentation.	I am playful, and jump into adventure with both feet.
My shower because it is hot and steamy.	I love erotic sex.
I love the **turquoise water** of the Caribbean.	I enjoy a romantic setting and love the props that activate the senses.
My swimming pool because I love to swim naked in the rain.	I am free and comfortable with my body during sex.

Do any of these answers resonate for you? Can you compare your own answers and discover more about your inner girl within? Can your answers be different tomorrow? Yes! Identities are constantly shedding their old skin to reveal the freshness underneath. Your feelings about yourself are always changing because you are growing from your problems, losses, possessions, successes, and conversations; from books, movies, and the different people in your life. Just revisit a movie or book you saw or read ten years ago; you will view it with different eyes.

The Slippery Slope of Self-Esteem

If you have trouble reviving the hidden girl within, you might be experiencing the common symptoms of low self-esteem. These symptoms may start slowly but then gradually spread to all aspects of your life—not just the obvious, such as when having to speak in public or ask for a long-overdue raise, but to all your relationships, especially the one you have with your spouse. Are you shy about expressing yourself physically in the bedroom and asking to be fulfilled according to your desires?

TALES OF STRESS ADDICTION
Laura's Travels

Laura loves to hike in Arizona. In fact, Laura loves to travel all over the world and is currently working as a travel editor of an e-magazine, even though she worked as a physicist for many years—a career she didn't choose for herself. Through her travels, she is exploring the world and meeting interesting people—one of them, herself. "After two husbands, three children, teaching physics, and running a business, I am finally at age sixty finding out who I am. That's why I love to travel alone and walk through different countries. I wasn't happy for many years, but I didn't understand why. After all these years, I'm finally coming to terms with who I am and what I want for myself. Well, better late than never."

Self-esteem is a slippery slope, and once you start sliding down, it is hard to return to your high point of feeling good about yourself—at least if you try to ascend by the same route you took on the way down. This is usually the biggest mistake. There are other, more direct routes to get to that high point. For example, suppose that during a meeting your boss sarcastically rejects your suggestion, and you feel embarrassed. In the next meeting, fearful and a bit self-conscious, you play it safe and don't say anything. This pattern continues for a while. You start to worry about your image and try to ascend the slippery slope by the same route, expressing your opinion out of a feeling of desperation; unfortunately, you sound unnatural and awkward. A more direct route would be to focus on your work and do a great job, earning you accolades from your boss, which will repair your self-esteem. Once you regain your self-confidence, you will feel more comfortable about bringing up your ideas during meetings. Where do you stand on the slope of self-esteem?

Rate Your Self-Esteem

For each of the following questions, circle the appropriate intensity, where 0 = never, and 5 = most of the time.

1. When you pass by a mirror, do you tug at your clothes, pull in your stomach, and reapply your makeup?   0 1 2 3 4 5

2. When you fail at something you have worked hard on, do you feel inadequate, and experience trouble perceiving the failure as a learning experience?   0 1 2 3 4 5

3. Do you feel guilty about changing your doctor when the doctor proves to be incompetent or uncaring, and are you afraid to ask for your medical records?   0 1 2 3 4 5

4. Are you nervous at family gatherings when the conversation turns to you?   0 1 2 3 4 5

5. Do you feel that if you say no to a friend, you will not be liked?

0 1 2 3 4 5

6. Do you speak on the phone to a family member or friend even when it is not a good time for you?   0 1 2 3 4 5

7. Do you get upset when your child does not perform well in a sport or doesn't do well on an exam, even when your child is fine with it?   0 1 2 3 4 5

8. Do you envy other women?   0 1 2 3 4 5

9. When a colleague or friend constantly borrows small change or a dollar here and there, do you feel petty when asking to be repaid?   0 1 2 3 4 5

10. Are you critical of others?   0 1 2 3 4 5

Add up your score.

Score: ___

Interpret Your Results

 0–20: Congratulations! You have solid self-esteem.

21–40: You are a little unsure of yourself and too accommodating.

41–50: You are running low on self-esteem and are in danger of identity theft.

Tools to Build Your Self-Esteem

- **Rid yourself of emotional programming** that dictates ideals—the perfect spouse, the perfect job, perfect children. Emotional programming will limit your self-discovery and ruin your happiness. This kind of false perfectionism takes you away from who you are because you will never achieve the ideals. There's no such thing as perfect, and you know it.

Tips for Curing Stress Addiction
Vow to Express Your Real Self

Women who suppress their thoughts and feelings in their marriage are at an increased risk of premature death, according to a study published in *Psychosomatic Medicine*. In fact, self-silencers had a four times higher risk of dying than women who expressed their feelings during conflicts with their spouses. At the very least, they are prone to depression and irritable bowel syndrome.

Reap the overall health benefits of marriage by expressing your real self. Don't stifle that hidden girl within to avoid arguing. Clear the air and breathe freely. Conflict triggers change.

- **Stop criticizing others.** The degree to which we need to criticize others is a good barometer of how much we dislike ourselves. Appreciate the people in your life for all their good points, and you'll learn to speak to yourself more kindly too. Stop yourself, even in midsentence, when you are judging someone negatively. Go the opposite route and keep complimenting people.

- **Take off your mask.** You say yes when you mean no. You try to please others, hoping that you will be liked. In short, you hide who you really are behind a mask. That's why the people in your life are surprised and confused when you remove your disguise from time to time and they get a glimpse of your true self. For example, do you agree to go shopping with your girlfriends when you don't like shopping in stores? Do you always provide snacks for those endless soccer games? Imagine not wearing your mask. See how light you feel and how freely you breathe when you relate to others without it.

TALES OF STRESS ADDICTION

The Morning Rush

Tara used to be a vice president in a major PR firm. Now at home with the children, she felt down about herself. She compared herself to other high-powered mommies: here she was stuck baking cookies and checking first- and third-grade homework assignments. Although she used to run a highly organized office, her own household was out of control. During a workshop, the group suggested that she use some of her office management strategies at home. Tara started baking only on special holidays, and created a schedule with an office-type inbox for incoming homework and an out box for homework that was completed. No more crumpled papers and unsigned homework! In a follow-up session, Tara explained that she felt better about herself because a regular homework management system prevented a lot of stress. The children also improved academically. Then Tara heard from the other side of the "Mommy Wars"—those who were jealous of her staying home with the kids. Within that context, she was able to appreciate her contribution.

Rediscovering Your Hidden Strengths

It's time to explore your authentic self, the big idea behind who you are and who you want to be, not what others want you to be. You might rely on your intuition as a first step. However, many of you might not hear its sweet little voice just yet, or do not trust your own intuition. Therefore, you need to take a closer look at your "intellectual capital" and give it an enticing label. You are taking an active role to define yourself in order to connect emotionally and creatively with what you want out of life. This means focusing on your unique abilities. Ultimately you will implement them and keep stretching them to accommodate your new growth. When you build on your strengths, you become enthusiastic, revitalized. One of the perks is that when you accept yourself, others will too. Take a good look at what you love to do and what you're good at. Your sample list might look like this:

WHAT I ENJOY	WHAT I'M GOOD AT DOING
Gardening	Communicating
Traveling	Writing
Reading	Completing
Belly dancing	Working with a team
Theatre	Improvising recipes
Writing	Creating a unique look
Smiling	Cheering people up
Talking to people	Telling the truth
Shopping	Using my imagination
Playing with my children	No job is too small for me to do

Let's look at the intersecting points:

- **Creativity** appears on both lists. **Gardening, belly dancing, theatre, and writing** are creative things I love doing. **Writing, improvising recipes, creating a unique look,** and **using my imagination** are things I'm good at doing.

- **Good communication skills** appear on both lists. **Smiling, talking to people,** and **playing with my children** are things I love doing. **Communicating, writing, cheering people up, working well with others,** and **telling the truth** are things I am good at doing.

- **Compassion** appears on both lists. **Smiling** and **talking to people** are things I love doing. **Cheering people up** and **no job is too small for me** are things I am good at doing.

Looking at these two lists, you can see the motivation of a self-starter and the responsible nature of a completer. This person has a great imaginative capacity that she would like to use to serve the greater good. In order for her to be happy, she needs to express herself through hobbies, volunteer work, or a career. If she wanted to consider a new career, it would most likely involve speaking, writing, and approaching subjects from a different angle—for example, journalism, advertising, event planning, screenwriting, TV or radio production, teaching, sales, or marketing.

Take an Opinion Poll

In addition to listing your attributes on paper, ask your family, workers, and friends what they think you are good at. As you gather more information about yourself, you will be inspired to take chances. In the process, you might even discover a new career or reinvent what you do at home. Instead of letting your limitations define who you are, setting you up for irritable reactions, you will develop your *signature strengths* to encourage you to respond from your higher self. You begin to feel *important*.

Take Notes

Because you are embarking on an identity quest, you never know when true inspiration will strike, so be prepared. Carry a small notebook to jot down some big ideas. You might hear a few life-altering words or see a poster at the train station with an image that resonates for you.

For example, when my mother was diagnosed with an aggressive terminal illness, a colleague was trying to comfort me with a few kind words. He was talking, but all I heard was, "Blah, blah, blah." Suddenly, three words came through loud and clear: "Lower your expectations." He didn't mean that I should lower my standards or stop striving. What he did mean was that if my ex-

Tips for Curing Stress Addiction
Silencing Your Inner Critic

If you regularly talk down to yourself or internalize only the critical comments about your endeavors, you need to redirect your
focus. Most of us focus on what we don't have, or ruminate
about that single negative remark, forgetting about all the compliments we get. Try this: list all the compliments people give
you. Soon you will have a more accurate sense of self. And
when you speak to yourself, use quality words that cheer you on
to conceive, believe, and achieve.

pectations were unreasonable—for example, if I was expecting my
mother to be magically cured—I would be sadly disappointed.
Those three words helped me make room for appreciating my relationship with my mother in the present, while I could—the way
she is, not the way she used to be or the way I wanted her to be.

Recall Voices from Your Past

In addition to being attentive to the present, consider going the
opposite route: remember relationships from your past that made
a big impression on you. For example, think about those special
bonds that you forged with others who helped shape your consciousness and values. Remember those special teachers, friends,
teammates—people who knew the real you and helped you appreciate and enjoy life.

When you take the time to remember their words, you might
want to speak to them, literally or symbolically. Refresh their
effect on you by calling them up, sending them an e-mail, or at
least having an imaginary conversation with them about their
impact on you, even if they have passed away. Answer these
questions about the significant people you once knew:

What do they remember about you?

What would you tell them about yourself today?

What questions do you have for them, so they can advise you?

Count Your Blessings

If you are still finding it difficult to label your signature strengths and feeling that perhaps after all is said and done, there is nothing to distinguish you from others, take heart from the following seemingly ordinary attributes. Then write your own list of "ordinary-extraordinary" hidden assets or self-taught skills. Here

---

 Tips for Curing Stress Addiction
Empowerment Exercise

Think back to your last success. Go back as far in time as you need to, even childhood. Make sure it is a quantifiable, validated success—in other words, an accomplishment that other people have formally called a success. For example, maybe you earned the lead in the third-grade school play, ran a lucrative charity bake sale in high school, studied for your graduate degree while working, or bought a house while working two jobs and raising your daughter as a single mom.

Next, label the specific personality traits that helped you achieve this particular success. Try to come up with at least three attributes. Here are some suggestions: determination, tenacity, creativity, intellect, organization, enthusiasm, hard work, faith, optimism. Once you have itemized your personal qualities, recall them back to your present life. Use these traits, the ones that worked for you in the past, to fuel your next success. Begin to consciously implement them today in your daily life. These are your gifts.

are some examples of the gifts that you might want to appreciate about your real self, that part of you that bubbles up when no one else is looking:

- I start friendly conversations with people I don't know, in the supermarket, on the train, or in a doctor's waiting room.

- I tell it like it is.

- I'm spontaneous and see the funny side of things even when things aren't apparently funny, making people laugh.

- I'm always on time.

- I do the job even when it's not my responsibility; I double-check.

- I don't complain.

- I'm a great listener.

If you still can't pinpoint your gifts or how to share them, keep asking your close friends and the colleagues you trust—and don't forget your kids, who are always watching you and will give it to you straight. Brainstorm periodically and watch your list expand.

Own Your Attribute

After you have gathered all this information about yourself, a pattern will emerge. A good way to clarify the gift in your own mind, cutting away to the essence to make it easy to grasp, is to write your own "business card" with your name and a brief description of your gift or your personal message—for example, Sara Johnson, *de-cluttering specialist*; Lucy Deane, *captain of my ship*; or Eilene Connor, *magical gardener*.

If you prefer speaking your truth, another choice for self-definition is to create a phone message describing the real you that people have missed. "You have reached Debbie Mandel, transformational artist. Sorry to have missed your call."

Stand Up and Take Responsibility

From this moment on, stop blaming your spouse, your children, your parents, and your coworkers for your personal unhappiness. Assume responsibility because you are *gifted*. When you know what you uniquely bring to the table, you will begin to perceive your spouse as a teammate and your friends as your support system.

Giving Birth to Yourself Again and Again

In the quest for your hidden girl within, you can cast away the aspects of your stress-filled life that are causing you unhappiness, as a more spirited version of yourself emerges.

At the Costa Rican butterfly farm I mentioned at the beginning of the chapter, I was fortunate to find a caterpillar and butterfly on the same leaf. It seemed as if the past and future were looking at one another: what was and what will be. This magical moment inspired me to be proud of my ancestry and the beliefs that shaped me, while I shed the old, worn-out narrative—the story of the stressed-out *martyr*—to give birth to my newest self.

When stressful events and obligations increase in our lives, we tend to destabilize and lose our sense of self. However, when our identity is intact, our vital energy somehow knows to balance and reset itself. To become more conscious of your individual identity, it helps to draw an analogy between the four stages of the birth process and identity transformation:

- In the womb: floating aimlessly

- Head engaged in the birth canal: stuck

Tips for Curing Stress Addiction
No More Arguing About Household Chores

Knowing how to assess your own worth brings added value to your marriage. You can run your marriage like a smoothly operating family business. Your spouse excels and specializes in _____. You excel and specialize in _____. Together as a team, yet separate in your skill sets, what wings can you give your dreams?

- Powerful contractions pushing the baby out: angry and sobbing

- Breathing on your own: light, free, and individual

We have all floated aimlessly and felt stuck or angry in our lives. These are not stages to be judged as negative, for they are part of a natural progression that ultimately leads to powerful new growth and rebirth. Which stage describes you today? Are you floating, or do you feel stuck? Inhale and exhale deeply to your own natural rhythm, embrace your separateness, and bask in your inner light.

Look Out for You

Periodically check in with yourself to evaluate what you are feeling and give yourself an identity tune-up with the following questions:

■ ■ ■

1. How do I really want to spend my time?

_____

_____

Tips for Curing Stress Addiction
Straighten Up to Straighten Out

We sit for many hours hunched over the computer or the steer-ing wheel. Not only does our posture suffer, stressing us physi-cally and emotionally, but the way we present ourselves to others is compromised. Try this quick exercise: bring your shoul-ders back and down, whether you are standing or sitting, to be in good postural alignment. This posture will immediately de-stress you and improve oxygen flow to your brain, which will facilitate clear, alert thinking. An added benefit is that others will reckon with what you have to say because of the way you present yourself: with your heart open and your back straight and proud.

2. How can I focus on what I need to do for myself rather than look to others to do things for me?

_____

_____

3. Is my kindness and generosity being taken advantage of? How often? By whom? Why?

_____

_____

4. Is the real me different from the person whom others see? What do others see? What do I really want them to see?

_____

_____

■ ■ ■

In the next chapter, you will learn how to nurture your nature. Get ready to strut your stuff!

STEP 3

Learn to Become a Healthy Narcissist

S tep 3 will show you how to celebrate your newly fortified identity by becoming a healthy narcissist.

"Healthy narcissist?" many people say when I mention the term. "How could any kind of narcissism be healthy?"

Both in myth and psychology, narcissism is perceived negatively, associated with self-centeredness, grandiosity, entitlement, arrogance, and manipulation. As a clinical disorder, narcissism tends to be more common in men (not a surprise), and as you recall from Step 1, men are generally happier than women. Hmm. Is there a connection? The clinical condition is an unhealthy extreme (and pathological narcissists are not happy people in private), but you can benefit from exploring what qualities are to be found in narcissism that might make you happy.

I'll tell you, and don't forget this: narcissism keeps the focus on you, which is precisely the point. This is about you, your life story, and that's the way it needs to be—not about anyone else.

As in the myth of Narcissus, seeing your reflection in the calm (de-stressed) water and embracing its beauty is a metaphor for appreciating your self, as long as you know how to swim. The problem with Narcissus was that he was not a healthy narcissist. In all versions of the myth, Narcissus dies unfulfilled; one of the most popular depicts him pining away over his reflection. Had he jumped into the water, Narcissus could have done some reality testing.

Poor guy. Too bad he didn't exercise. Swimming would have been a meaningful workout, a real lifesaver.

Healthy Narcissism Is an Acquired Trait

Most little girls aren't brought up to be healthy narcissists.

When you made positive or self-appreciating statements as a child, you probably heard from your parents, "Good little girls don't show off," or "It's rude to brag." And it was either overtly or subliminally transmitted to you that when other people complimented you, you were supposed to accept the compliment with great humility—even better would be to politely push the compliment away from you. Self-deprecation was the virtue you learned, not healthy, normal narcissism.

In fact, most of the time when I compliment an adult woman: "You look amazing in that outfit," the most common response I get is "Nah, I have to lose weight," or "You look great too!" Rarely do I get an unqualified "Thank you." In contrast, when I compliment a man, the predominant response is "Yeah, thanks."

As you internalize this "don't show off," self-deprecating female identity, you begin to believe ultimately that you have nothing to show off about. You try harder. You grow into the mind-set of an anxious-to-please woman to validate your self-worth. Consequently, you serve others all the time, hoping to hear what a good girl you are. That's why you have to relearn how to be gloriously, naturally narcissistic, the way you once were as a young, free-spirited child—before you were taught this etiquette of true-self suppression.

Narcissism as a Positive Attribute

A healthy narcissist is not better looking than you, but she will act *as if* by strutting her stuff. A healthy narcissist enjoys being the center of attention but doesn't demand to be so every second of the day. Most of the time there is nothing special about a narcissist, no distinguishing ability, only a satisfied sense of true self.

A healthy narcissist simply assumes that she deserves more out of life and goes after it. She believes that she has the inalienable right to her own happiness and that when she is happy, other people—especially her family—will be happier too. Does it sound like this kind of happiness could work for you?

Tips for Curing Stress Addiction
Too Much of a Good Thing

When thirty-eight-year-old Dana entered the room, I could see that her appearance had changed drastically over the course of the month since I'd seen her last. Her body looked haggard. Her face had deeper lines than I remembered. Instead of her free-flowing beautiful blonde curls, her hair was straight and severely tied back. "I don't seem to have any energy, and I'm achy all over. Can you motivate me?" After answering a few key questions, Dana proudly stated that she worked out seven days a week, from eight in the morning until noon, then returned to the gym for a one-hour spin class in the evening.

"Motivate you? No way. You need to do less, not more. All this exercise—instead of reaping the benefits, you're exhausted and depressed."

Dana was shocked because she had expected exercise to give her a wild rush of feel-good chemistry, along with the perk of eating anything she wanted—which she clearly didn't do.

"What's really going on with you?" I asked.

Dana explained that her art gallery was depleting her personal coffers, and she needed some fresh new talent to rent space. "Also, many of the female artists in their twenties have these amazing, waif-like bodies; I'm so old. And when I went to the gym to do something about my body, I got sucked into the madness along with the other crazies who work out all morning."

"Dana . . . you'd look better if you let your face relax into a smile and let your body rest for a few days. You're good enough!"

I negotiated a workout regimen that was acceptable to Dana, one hour six days a week—to begin after a week's hiatus. A couple of months later, Dana's skin was glowing; she could have been one of the artworks. Also, her gallery was turning a profit. She'd given up her self-defeating all-day stress routine and practiced some healthy narcissism.

To meet her need for attention and to get what she wants, a healthy narcissist knows how to be charming and positive, a kind of queen bee. And she is on the right track, because people buzz around positive and witty people. Observe the water cooler at work. Who is the center of attention? And how about the kitchen table at home? A healthy narcissist's upbeat disposition, a veritable powerhouse, generates more of her own positive energy in response to people's adoration, as others interact with her and even seek her out. People usually try to feel better about their daily life and look for any opportunity to absorb some positive energy to drive their day. Her popularity reinforces her status in her own eyes. Because a healthy narcissist assumes that she is well liked and has something meaningful to contribute, she feels comfortable delegating tasks and responsibilities to make her life easier, freeing herself to recharge her energy and fulfill herself. Others are glad to take on those responsibilities because they enjoy orbiting around her.

Create Yourself

According to Zen philosophy and other spiritual practices, you have to consider that everything good has something bad in it and everything bad has something good in it in order to establish a harmonious balance in daily life. Let's apply this to narcissism versus unselfish giving.

Unselfish giving and humility are noble; however, they do have their darker side: giving yourself away and not taking care of yourself. Psychologists use the term narcissism to describe self-absorbed individuals who feel entitled to all kinds of things. But what's good about narcissism is that you hold the fundamental belief that you deserve the best and are worthy of love and respect. As a result, you take care of your appearance, dress for success, exercise, eat right, and carve out the time to do the things you love doing. You are inspired to hold yourself in high esteem to cultivate traits like good posture and honest conversation. For many of us who have been brought up to be self-effacing and self-deprecating, this means casting away the old self and creating a new one, as we've seen in Step 2. And in rediscovering that hidden girl within, we acknowledge the need for a degree of self-centered, self-appreciating, healthy narcissism.

George Eliot aptly said, "It's never too late to become what you might have been." Unleash your imagination and create a new personal narrative. "It's just a wishful kind of self-imagination," you might say, but the point is that it is *your* self-imagination, and within this new way of presenting yourself and behaving with others are some of the deepest truths about yourself—what you wish for and what you aspire to be.

Healthy Role Models

There are so many wonderful healthy narcissists—actors, painters, writers, professors, surgeons, judges, CEOs, and politicians—who have developed more expansive personalities even if they didn't start out with such public self-confidence. If they didn't have a narcissistic streak, they would never have had the guts to cut out the shy, modest, or self-effacing personalities of their childhood and put themselves out there in the public eye to climb the ladder of success. Every professor lecturing to a class, standing in the front of the room with all eyes on her, is a bit of a narcissist. Surgeons are known in the medical field for their God complex. Every writer who publishes a book is a narcissist too—I plead guilty. Imagine the presumption of my thinking that people really need to listen to what I have to say.

In all these cases people have believed in their dreams and set goals for themselves. This belief has propelled them to rise to challenges. They like themselves, delight in their achievements, and respect others. Similarly, you have to believe in yourself to make others believe in you too. It's not bragging—well, maybe it is just a little. It's owning your gift and sharing it with others because you believe that you have something worthwhile to contribute.

TALES OF STRESS ADDICTION

The Story of Two Narcissists

It was rush hour on the Long Island Railroad in New York. A woman about seven months pregnant stood holding on to the pole along with me and a few others for a forty-five minute ride into Manhattan. In close proximity sat a well-dressed man with his attaché case on the seat next to him. I knew he hadn't bought a ticket for his attaché case, and couldn't believe that the guy left this very pregnant woman standing while his case took up an empty seat. I motioned to her to sit down, but she was shy and said softly, "Never mind. It's all right." That upset me even more, so I finally turned to the man and said very loudly over the sound of the train, "Excuse me, sir, could you take the attaché case off the seat next to you so this expectant mother can sit down?" Instead of apologizing or making some humorous comment about being absentminded, he glared at me and put the briefcase on the floor with clear contempt and reluctance—obviously a true narcissist. I practically shoved the young woman into the seat.

Of course, being a stress management specialist who instantly analyzes my own behavior, I felt right away that I was being pretty narcissistic myself. Who was I to ride in on my white horse of self-righteousness and push around the by now quite embarrassed young woman against her will? Wasn't that grandiose and a bit selfish of me, too? I wanted her to assume her rightful place as a healthy narcissist, but it was I who was actually doing the work, not she. She whispered a sweet thank you to me, and I hope to this day that the benefits of what I thought was my own healthy narcissism outweighed her discomfort. But I know for sure there were at least two competing narcissists on the train that day.

A Gift from God?

Take a closer look at the cliché you used to describe a narcissistic guy you once dated: "He thinks he's God's gift to women!" In a sense, didn't that self-assessment give him the courage to call you and interact with you? Isn't he a special gift to someone out there? When a baby is born, we might say, "This infant is a precious gift from God." When the baby grows up, is that adult no longer a gift from God? What if you strutted around with a bit of a swagger empowered by your belief that you are God's gift? Would there be more adventures you would experience or people you would interact with because you have faith in your ability and are proud of who you are? Would you let anyone take advantage of your time and space? Would you settle for living a contracted life?

Do Clothes Make the Woman?

Narcissists want to look good for themselves. When you take care of your appearance—not for your man, your girlfriends, or your colleagues, but for yourself—you feel more confident and attractive.

That's why you need a few outfits that through color, style, and fit give shape to your unique inner self; you want to make that entrance whether it is the school lunch room, the office, or your family room. While you're at it, remember to express yourself in the way you carry yourself, how you walk and toss your hair, the pressure of your touch when you shake hands, and how you look people in the eye. Cultivate distinction.

Claire, a trader in a hedge fund, explains, "I love to wear jewelry and make a special choice every day. It can be inexpensive costume jewelry. It's not about showing off to clients about how well I am doing at work. Jewelry adorns my personality. I like to express myself in this creative way."

Tips for Curing Stress Addiction
How Would a Healthy Narcissist Say It?

You say, "I'm so flighty. It's like I have adult ADD."
The healthy narcissist says, "I'm a scanner. I'm good at so many things and am looking for what I really enjoy."

You say, "I'm disgusted with my big belly hanging over my jeans."
The healthy narcissist says, "I'm voluptuous and substantial. Anyway, do I want to be remembered ultimately for how thin I was?"

You say, "That salesgirl is so abrupt with me. She doesn't like me."
The healthy narcissist says, "She's having a hard day. It's not me, it's her."

Your personal style creates a sensory impression expressing who you are. For example, if you always wear black, you might be expressing that you are a minimalist, free of clutter and a bit mysterious. In contrast, if you always wear bright colors with large pieces of jewelry, you are saying, "Look at me! I am free, expansive, and uninhibited."

When you are depressed, you are likely to sit in pajamas all day, not paying attention to your hair or putting on a little makeup. Wearing sweats day in and day out, wondering why your husband is no longer noticing you, means that you are not paying attention to yourself. Getting dressed each day transmits a statement that you have made up your mind to be happy, reinforcing who you are to yourself or creating the self you wish to be! Putting on different costumes is like trying on different identities for size and experimenting with different parts of your personality to see what image you wish to create or resurrect. You don't have to wait for Halloween to have fun.

Beyond Appearance

But it's not all about how you look. Who you are is also bound up in your abilities, education, productivity, and relationships. That's why healthy narcissists don't spend all day exercising but also take the time to improve their minds, fuel their brains, and enjoy their most intimate relationships. We'll talk about expanding and nurturing your libido and sexual life in Step 6, but for now let's not forget how many classes and special training courses you could take to pursue creative gifts, workplace ambitions, and better relationships.

Essentially, healthy narcissism means that you do things for yourself because they support your identity. You are an ambassador of your own world. When people mention your name and talk about you, they identify you with your personal message: "She always says . . ." "She is always good at . . ." "She always makes me feel like I'm the most . . ."

Because status is important to a narcissist, special possessions enhance and transmit that status both to herself and to others who need to be made aware of her new position. Now, I'm not suggesting that you become a crass materialist or feed into media-driven consumerism and wreak havoc with the household budget for food and rent. Rather, use your personal possessions to anchor your ever-changing identity, which may be expanding in many directions. This means that you take a second look at what you have buried in the closet, or get some simple items that make a big statement about who you are both physically and spiritually.

Because my identity is constantly transforming as I love to explore and reinvent, which is my creative process, sometimes I wonder if my visual message and my verbal message are clearly in synchrony. Recently I heard my name used as a verb, "You have been Debbie Mandeled!" "Oh, what do you mean by that?" I asked. I wear many hats and wondered which one of my qualities

Tips for Curing Stress Addiction
Create Your Spiritual Totem Pole

Totem poles were tall, colorful wood carvings sculpted by Native Americans to symbolize wealth, status, family identity, and personal stories, monuments that identified and glorified soul-stirring moments. Create a small version of a totem pole on your desk to serve as a reminder or inspiration to yourself to become more of who you are, to give structure to your inner life. Your totem pole doesn't have to be vertical. Think about the colors you like, the animals or plants that inspire you. What you are drawn to in nature will provide clues to what you long for at home and at work—how to live more naturally, in tune with your own nature. The Indians drew great energy from the earth and the sky. They found counterparts in nature even to use as names to live up to. Because I am an avid, Monet-type gardener and a bit uninhibited as far as personality goes, my friends call me "Princess Wildflower." And I do try to have wildflowers on my desk at all times.

To create your totem pole, take a few moments to really look at a neighborhood tree, listen to a bird, or feel the sun on your skin. If your attention is drawn to a flower, what color and what stage of blossoming attracts you most? If you prefer a more pragmatic symbol, you can choose a miniature car or boat to display. Perhaps you would enjoy using your visual cue as a screen-saver, including sound for greater synergy (this is not the eighteenth century). Sitting on my desk is a photograph of a honey bee on a pink rose, and a four-inch hand holding a pair of silver dumbbells.

was being invoked. It's always a good idea to get a reality check as to how others perceive you. "It means let's look at the positive side, the sunny side of the street; you know, Debbie Mandeled." That works for me!

Why Women Need to Like Themselves

For men, courage and self-respect are the driving forces behind their relationships and behavior at home or at work. For women, the motivation is more about getting along and being liked by others.

Much of this difference is grounded in brain anatomy. Testosterone makes men more aggressive and insistent in their quest for status, also known as respect. The female brain has a deeper

TALES OF STRESS ADDICTION
What Women Can Learn from Male Coworkers

Barbara, a vice president of a large marketing firm, cannot believe how the women in her department who do excellent work do not ask for raises or promotions. In contrast, the male employees, some not as capable as their female coworkers, regularly demand increases in status and compensation. I asked Barbara if she rewarded the women with bonuses and promotions. "I wish I could, but if they don't ask for it, my hands are tied, as I am on the management side. I just want to shake some sense into them: speak up and demand what you are worth! The men who have an inflated value of themselves are making more money than the humble ladies, just because they demand it."

limbic system, which is wired to the need to be well liked. However, you already know that people pleasing comes at a high cost.
As a natural people pleaser due to biology and culture, a woman
sets herself up for stress in all her relationships. Being popular
often means giving a great deal away to others—unless you are a
narcissist.

Note that pleasers and givers have plenty of needy takers
lined up with their arms outstretched and hands open. But being
such a crowd pleaser creates an underground hot spring of resentment because there's such an inequity about this kind of presentation. Health and happiness depend on homeostasis, and in this
case homeostasis is the balance between giving and receiving.
There's no way you can be cheerful at all times if you remain just
a giver to others, and if you appear so it's a fake.

Be aware that when you are always doing things for others,
the tendency on their part is to expect it, take it for granted, or,
even worse, consider all this kindness and generosity a sign of
weakness! That's where women can learn from men about elevating their status—to hold themselves in high esteem. As a

 Tips for Curing Stress Addiction
CEO of the House

In traditional marriages, husbands are often described as the
providers because they bring home sufficient money to sustain
the household. However, in this same traditional household
where a woman does not work outside the home, she too is a
provider, nurturing, feeding, cleaning, and decorating. Balance
the two providers on a scale, and clearly a woman provides more
services. And if a wife works outside the home too, then her side
of the scale doesn't just tip, but crashes to the bottom with a
thud. Recognize your status and claim your R&R. Provide for
yourself.

healthy narcissist, you will value yourself and be popular without giving yourself away. Your positive confidence will shine through you, and others will gravitate to the whole you, not the part you give away.

Put On Your Pink Tiara

I'll bet you never envisioned how your life would be today while you were planning your wedding day, thrilled about wearing a gorgeous gown and a tiara with a white veil. At some point (you're not quite sure when it happened), the romantic movie where you played the part of the heroine was switched off, and some neorealistic film noir of suffering and anguish was substituted instead. I'm here to remind you that it is time to put back on your tiara!

My daughter, Amanda, taught me this lesson on her sixteenth birthday, a ritual celebration of youthful narcissism.

Amanda was enjoying every moment of this frilly rite of passage. Celebrating her metamorphosis with ten girlfriends, she turned to me an hour before we had to leave for the restaurant and smiled demandingly, "I almost forgot! I need a tiara, and we have to get it now!"

Thinking she wanted some designer jewelry headgear, I replied, "Who do you think you are, the Queen of England?"

"Mom, it costs about $1.50, and you can get it at the party store."

"Oh well, in that case you can have two!"

"And Mom, can you get some nonalcoholic champagne and some of those plastic fluted champagne glasses and serve it to my friends outside in the backyard when we return?"

At that moment, I realized that my daughter knew how to create, direct, get what she needs, and have fun doing it. I had a lot to learn from her.

As per instructions, I greeted my daughter's friends with bubbling nonalcoholic champagne while she went to her room, donned her next outfit for the evening, and made her appearance wearing a pink tiara, laughing heartily as she greeted me and her entourage. Oh, I forgot to mention: I was also wearing mine— remember, I bought two!

Tips for Curing Stress Addiction
The Goddess Walk

One blue Monday in March, I was about to begin a stress management workshop when I looked around the room at twenty-five women and four men, and everyone appeared downright miserable. I wondered if there was something in the air: Had the ozone layer deteriorated even more than usual, or had some bad news been broadcast on TV that I didn't know about yet? No, everyone was either irritable for his or her own private reasons, or the negativity had begun with one member and infected everyone else. I had to regroup. I began the session differently than I had planned.

"Stand up, everyone, and let's do a goddess walk, and you guys over there walk like gods." People stood up and looked at me as if I was crazy. "Yes, keep your chin up and stand up straight and, most important, don't suck in your belly—let it all hang out. Now strut your stuff. I want to see a swagger in your walk." I led the way, exaggerating my walk like someone who owned the streets. They followed me, walking around the room in a snakelike fashion. "Now nod a greeting to everyone you meet on this walk. Smile and acknowledge each other like a goddess or god with the power to do anything she wants and just move on." Everyone was laughing hysterically. A few minutes later, when we sat down to discuss our issues, Nancy began, "Goddesses, huh! This is the best session we ever had! When I get home, I will be a goddess. When I go to work, I will be a goddess. Whenever I walk, I will be a goddess."

How to Go from People Pleaser to Self-Pleaser

To be a healthy narcissist, you'll need to leave the comfort zone of a stress-addicted woman and create a new and bolder true self.

Step out on the ledge and go to the edge. Liberate yourself from your self-imposed, self-limiting and safe role. Because you have never done it before, it's time to leap like a ballerina or hike up a mountain, first in your imagination and then in your concrete reality.

As Maya Angelou says, "If one is lucky, a solitary fantasy can totally transform one million realities."

Channel Your Energies

Think it and do it. As an adrenaline junkie, you thrive on accomplishment. Therefore, channel your energy into personal challenges that help you accomplish for yourself. Experience the exhilaration of doing something that requires you to leave your good-little-girl comfort zone—ziplining, learning how to tango, or starting a new business—and that serves no other purpose than amazing yourself: *look what I did; look what I can do.*

There is another benefit to challenging yourself, which involves learning how to decompress. The stress of a challenge that is under your control, that you in fact initiated, helps you raise your threshold for future destabilizing experiences. Here's how this works. You choose the challenge and then you conquer it, which makes you feel confident and proud. You realize that you can successfully handle this type of stress and file this memory away for when a new stressor comes your way. Sometimes unexpected waves hit you in quick succession, so it is important to prepare for life's instabilities, learning how to swim away or to keep afloat until help arrives. You need to challenge your balance all the time, rehearsing to become more flexible and fluid in your personal narrative and preparing for stressful situations during the good times, not when obstacles come along and you feel panicky. Store up those moments of self-confident mastery, the relaxation response experience, to increase your ability to cope with stress. Here are some suggestions:

- Dare to be a bit outrageous. That means changing up your predictable routine. If you hear people saying, "What's gotten into you?" you're on the right track.

- Go the opposite route when your balance is upset. For example, if something destructive happens in your life, go the creative route to restore your balance. Put something back in your life. If you have too much on your plate and are suffering from the excess, then balance it out by letting things go.

- When you exercise, work on your core, the center of your gravity. For example, if you stand on a balance

Tips for Curing Stress Addiction
The Dreaded Family Gathering

Around the holidays, people become upset contemplating getting together with family members who make them feel uncomfortable by pushing their buttons. There is always someone who interrogates, dispenses unwanted advice, or makes sarcastic remarks like "Put on some weight lately?" "Still haven't finished your master's degree?" "Isn't it time you had a baby?" This is the best time to act like a healthy narcissist. Smile and say nothing. Goddesses don't always answer. Distract and deflect the conversation with the latest movie or book, or bring along a magazine others will like. Prepare a witty story in advance to amuse them. Move on to their favorite topic of conversation—themselves.

pod, Bosu ball, or thick foam, you feel wobbly. You need to stabilize your legs, drawing power from the middle of your body as you keep your eyes focused straight ahead. Walking on uneven pavement becomes a piece of cake, and so do other unbalancing things in your life. See Step 4 for more tips on healthy exercise.

Toss the Toxicity

Perhaps the biggest impediment to cultivating healthy narcissism is guilt. Looming above us is The Standard, and we have not lived up to it. Whose standard is it? We don't exactly know. All we know is that we don't measure up. We are susceptible to feeling guilty because guilt has deep archetypal roots as ancient as the Bible. While growing up, we were made to feel guilty for real transgressions, for which we were taught to apologize and make amends, instilling a sense of right and wrong based on social and religious upbringing.

Tips for Curing Stress Addiction
Is This Really True?

- I am responsible for everyone's happiness. If my children, spouse, and parents are not happy, it's my fault.

- I must respond to *their* requests, even when doing so violates my own needs.

- Whatever went wrong is my fault.

- If I don't comply with my family's, friend's, or colleague's demands, they will do desperate things.

- I must not enjoy myself during a period of mourning or loss. If I have fun during this time, I am not grieving properly.

- If my kids mess up, it's my fault, no matter how old they are.

However, we were also taught to feel guilty when we expressed our individuality, when we ever behaved the slightest bit
like nonconformists in the conformist world of school and religion. Perhaps we questioned a teacher's interpretation and were
reprimanded for questioning authority. Or, studying classical
piano, we burst into an original song that we composed. Many of
us fidgeted in our seats in a house of worship as we prayed that
the service would end, while the priest, minister, or rabbi stared
us down. This kind of guilt is stifling to identity.

In fact, many of our guilty feelings are a cover-up for low self-
esteem. To sum up: there is a right and wrong way to feel guilty:

- The **right way** is to face your guilt head on by
  observing the problem, solving the problem, and
  challenging any irrational thoughts of how bad you
  are; if you are not in fact responsible for the problem, you pass it on to its rightful owner.

- The **wrong way** is to dwell on it, beat yourself up
  about it, and restrict yourself to activities of atone-
  ment to prove to everyone else that you are a good
  person.

As a result of these guilty thoughts, you overwork, become
overly conscientious, close your emotions off, and engage in self-
denial to make amends. You become locked into the status quo,
not daring to do things differently because you are afraid of being
wrong. And besides, you can't handle criticism.

When addicted to stress, you are very sensitive. You are absolutely, positively right most of the time—you have to be. For
if you are wrong, you will feel guilty, and as a woman you feel
your guilt intensely, which makes you depressed, perpetuating the
whole nasty cycle. Guilt stifles your spontaneous responses to life
and erodes your sense of worth. With all this guilt in your head

TALES OF STRESS ADDICTION

Please, You Just Have to Be There for Me

Beth was getting married on the beach in Jamaica over a four-day weekend in January. She invited her friend Melissa to come along with a few other close friends. However, Melissa declined, as this was not a good time for her to leave work, and she needed to be home to supervise her children's high school finals. She explained to Beth that she would celebrate with the happy couple when they returned. After all, this was Beth's second marriage, and they were in their mid-forties.

Beth was furious. "You are my best friend. How can you not stand up for us? We just left our former spouses, and this wedding is the highlight of all our tribulations." Beth proceeded to cry. Melissa agreed to go, feeling guilty that if she didn't go, it meant she didn't approve of the relationship. Her children were upset; her husband thought Melissa was being manipulated, and besides, he didn't approve of Beth's having cheated on her husband. Melissa felt like the taut rope in a tug of war. Then Beth had a fight with her fiancé, and he called off the wedding. Melissa received a note of cancellation, as one of a mass e-mail. After that, Beth didn't answer Melissa's phone calls or e-mails. Melissa realized that she had been used. Apparently Beth knew how to make Melissa feel guilty when she needed her. Beth, the unhealthy narcissist, had trumped Melissa, who was still learning to be a healthy narcissist.

there is no room for your dreams. However, don't feel guilty about feeling guilty. You need guilt to fuel the dysfunctional habit of stress addiction.

Ugh! Let's not keep going back there again. Repeat after me: NO MORE TOXIC GUILT. Be a confident, well-balanced, well-prepared, healthy narcissist.

Develop Healthy Confidence

Healthy narcissists do not have overwhelming feelings of guilt. They have a reasonably positive opinion of their intelligence and capabilities, which makes them adept at advocating for themselves. And should they make a mistake, they don't dwell on it, but say, "I'll do better next time."

In fact, from their perspective, they are doing the best they can. Objectively, they direct their attention to and analyze the external circumstances that have created the problem—rather than wallowing in self-blame. They are able to separate who they are from what they do, which helps them learn and grow. Narcissists are inspired to seek opportunities where they can shine, and they therefore move quickly away from past failure to restore their self-confidence or to reinvent themselves to shine in another way.

In sharp contrast to a healthy narcissist stands a stressed-out woman who always feels guilty about what she ought to be doing and who constantly needs emotional support to validate her. Are you that woman? Does your spouse need to be careful of everything he says to you, always hoping that you are in a good mood, always prefacing his requests with a compliment? This can be an overwhelming burden. When you develop more narcissistic attributes, you become more secure and confident, no longer perceiving yourself as a doormat and certainly not acting like one. When you become more self-ish (of the self), tending to your own needs, everyone around you relaxes and benefits from your increased vitality and genuine cheerfulness. In turn, you stop making them feel guilty that they did not read your mind, because you clearly ask for what you want, just as any self-respecting narcissist would. *The formula for a guilt-free, healthy narcissist: I do for me = I do for us.*

How to Survive Friendly Fire

Women are complex creatures, and so follow our friendships. Although our friends mean everything to us, serving as our support system, our confidantes and playmates, they can also house contradictions like jealousy and betrayal—as we do for them. Many of us believe that female friendships should go the distance, especially if there is a history. After all, they are praised on talk shows and idealized in magazines, and as a result we are reluctant to end these friendships when they become toxic or bring out the worst in us. We think that there is something wrong with us and dismiss our true feelings. We don't like to admit to these internal struggles between social convention and our individuality, which inevitably build up to the question, Do I stay or do I go? You are the only one who knows the answer to this question, but consider those options that allow you to be more authentic and open about your true feelings. If a friend pushes your buttons, reflect on what within yourself you wish to fulfill. Even if you must shed a friend or two along the way, you make room for new, more uplifting relationships.

The Green-Eyed Monster

Women tend to feel jealous when they compare themselves to other women, regarding appearance, accomplishments, children, home, and husband. There is nothing to feel guilty about if you feel jealous. It is a normal emotion because human beings are competitive creatures, especially when they feel that they are missing something other people have.

However, if you are always camped outside at a distance, spying and fantasizing about the good fortune of your friends, then you are not using your gifts or transforming yourself. You are stuck in a negative self-perception. Typically, envy paints a larger-than-life picture of other people's accomplishments and lifestyles. How can one possibly find peace in her heart?

Healthy narcissists, however, are not jealous—at least for long. They use jealousy as a catalyst for growth and to get what they need. Let's look at this process more closely.

Let's say that you reason that you are more deserving than the object of your jealousy because you are smarter, more talented, more beautiful, more experienced. And you might be. However, the problem with your reasoning is that deep down inside, you don't really believe that you possess any of those qualities, and that's why you are jealous in the first place! You doubt that you will ever attain what others have—the glory, the romance, or the lifestyle.

What are you going to do about it? Pray that the object of your envy loses it all, so that you will look better in contrast? No, that won't accomplish anything.

Instead, turn your jealousy around and transform it into a stepping-stone to the next level of achievement. Study the object of your envy and imitate her. Obviously she has the secret formula—go out and learn it. Next, customize this formula to resonate with your own signature strengths. Get creative and give it your personal stamp.

Try this: ask the person you want to be like to help you out with advice or networking. (Notice how easily jealousy can be reconceptualized!) A healthy narcissist wouldn't hesitate to ask for this kind of help, not just once but again and again. A healthy narcissist hangs out with the best and most useful people.

If You Are the Object of Envy

Congratulations! Don't feel inhibited about owning your success. I'm not saying that you should rub people's faces in it, but don't be afraid to delight in what you have accomplished simply out of fear that others will be jealous.

Be mindful of others' jealousy, and don't fuel it. However, be aware that you could subtly absorb their disapproval; you might be tempted to use people's jealousy as an excuse to further withdraw and limit your spirit, to revert to past behavior in childhood where you were taught not to show off.

As in aversion therapy, the more you accept a few jealous "remarks" or looks, the more accustomed you will become to neutralizing them. Key to this process is taking a stance of compassionate understanding. Try making the jealous person feel good. Be generous with a compliment, and you can both share the limelight like two healthy narcissists. Unlike a clinical narcissist who needs to shine solo, a healthy narcissist enjoys the company of like-minded successful people.

Recognizing a Toxic Friendship

Watch out for explicit or hidden toxicity from people who do not have your best interests at the heart of their own narcissism.

- If your friend speaks to you sarcastically and most of her remarks, though housed in humor, are basically insulting, put a stop to it by expressing your displeasure.

- If you are sick, have lost your job, or are having marital problems, and your friend keeps asking you for the smallest, most intimate details about your condition, separate your identity from that of your plight, and get back into life. This friend is fascinated by your misfortune as if watching a house on fire yet

TALES OF STRESS ADDICTION

The Story of a Friendship Ending

Susan ended a very close friendship with a funny, charming, intelligent girlfriend named Rebecca. Evidently, in the heat of the moment when she needed to vent, Susan had revealed a few too many choice details of some of the innocuous arguments she had once had with her husband, Bruce. But Susan's antennae perked as she began to hear increasingly sarcastic remarks from Rebecca about Bruce. "Then she started steering me to girls' nights out where she would flirt with various men—basically her night out from living her own unhappy life. I felt uncomfortable, like she was manipulating me away from Bruce. I noticed that I began to get stomachaches when I was with her. Since I am a direct person, I told her straight out that she was undermining me and my marriage and that our friendship was no longer working for me." Rebecca blew up. Next she sent a cute *Sorry* card and after that a little gift, a coffee cup painted with the words *I miss you*. Finally, Rebecca rang Susan's doorbell. "May I come in? I was just being real with you, can't you let it go?" Susan replied, "Yes, I do want to let it go, but I don't think we can be on the same level of friendship any more. I don't like your reality and the effect it has on me." Since then, Susan has sat near other people during parties and luncheons, greeting Rebecca politely but remaining cool and distant. "I forgave her in my heart, but moved on with my head."

doing nothing to put it out. Your friend sees you as an object of pity, but you need empowerment to heal. Saying "I would rather not talk about it" is a clear signal to your friend to back off.

- If your friend tries to monopolize your time, possess you, and limit your contact with others, then that friendship has become not only toxic but parasitic. Don't become enmeshed. Declare your independence.

- If your friend is self-absorbed, rarely complimenting you, manipulating you into doing what she wants by tugging at your heart strings, calling you when it is convenient only for her, even late at night, beware! You are being used and drained by an energy vampire—a real, clinical narcissist. Establish your boundaries. Her soap opera does not need to become your soap opera.

Show and Tell

When you are a healthy narcissist, you show and tell the world who you are, you reap the satisfaction of taking a stand, and you become a force to be reckoned with. As a healthy narcissist, you will have satisfying intimate relationships because you won't be afraid to make yourself vulnerable or to take a leap out of your comfort zone.

Inevitably, some people will line up behind you and others won't. But that's okay, because what's important is that you are in good alignment. Make your activities and relationships self-affirming, creating a golden circle of good energy around you and your friends. You will feel energized and stimulated, not tired or depleted from doing for others or worrying about them.

■ ■ ■

The next chapter gets to the heart of the matter—the components of self-care that emphasize the "health" in healthy narcissism. Read on to learn how food affects mood and how exercise can help you look and feel like a goddess.

Build a Healthy Body

S tep 4 will show you how you can eliminate stress addiction in your life by taking care of yourself physically, ensuring that you're operating at peak performance—healthy, happy, and optimistic.

This sounds like a no-brainer, right? All you have to do is eat right (as in less) and exercise. Not exactly rocket science. But . . .

As we all know, achieving and sustaining a fit, trim, and healthy body is one of the biggest problems most women struggle with daily. (A lot of men, too, but that's another story).

So let's take a closer look at this issue, which is so crucial to reducing stress and so closely related to every aspect of our lives: our relationships, our identity, healthy narcissism, self-destructive habits, our struggle for change. And don't forget that universal human desire to live as long as we can.

How Stress Addiction Is Bad for Your Health

When you are addicted to stress, you often skip meals and seldom exercise—who has the time?

The Stress-Addicted Approach to Food

Here's a typical stress addiction food scenario. You cut out breakfast intentionally, grab a bag of potato chips for lunch, then pig out on fast-food take-out for dinner. When you do eat, you wolf down food in the car or at your desk, and there's usually a cup of coffee in your hand to jolt your body into performing when it's running on empty. At best you eat standing up in your kitchen while you are doing something else, such as supervising homework. You don't taste your food or sense its texture.

Without connecting the cause to the effect, you wonder why you feel more stressed and depleted than ever. Perhaps you have also been experiencing mysterious stomachaches and heartburn. When stress levels go up, digestive problems like gastroesophageal reflux and irritable bowel syndrome tend to increase. On some level, our stress, which brings about our lack of self-care, is causing us to physically and emotionally digest ourselves.

Acts of Depression

Many stress-addicted women reach this point of frustration and say to themselves, "This is depressing. I'm feeling sick and achy, and I'm gaining weight. I'd better take some of those new, what do you call them, serotonin reuptake inhibitors. Yes, that's it. I need to raise my serotonin levels to improve my brain, increase my positive energy levels, be totally happy all the time."

Well, let me tell you, serotonin reuptake inhibitors may have their place when treating serious clinical depression, but be aware that for the general population, these mood elevators do not work as well as we are led to believe. Beware of those glossy ads showing people taking Prozac, Zoloft, or Paxil, then skipping through the grass or holding hands by the shore. I find it interesting that doctors who prescribe these medications so promiscuously also send their patients who are still not happy to classes and support groups. There are often such medicated but still stressed-out, unhappy individuals in my sessions or trainings, no matter their age or background.

That's why I always talk about nature's own stress management prescription: a balanced nutritional plan that includes specific mood-elevating foods, implemented together with the feel-good chemistry of exercise. Imagine the look on the faces of people who came to one of my programs thinking they were going to hear a motivational speech about being stuck in a bad mood and found themselves doing squats, calf raises, wall push-ups, and shoulder presses! And guess what? They felt exhilarated, energized—alive. This is the kind of science that can help you with your life story.

Gaining Balance Through Healthy Eating

What you eat, how you eat, how much you eat, and where you eat reflect your emotional state of mind or trigger it. You might feel that eating is involuntary and that you don't consciously think much about it, particularly when you are stressed and distracted by other things. However, eating is a selective process involving conscious decisions. You are just too busy to notice. By identifying your eating patterns—such as feasting mainly on processed foods, eating sizeable snacks at night in front of the TV, or skipping meals, particularly breakfast—you can overcome self-sabotaging, stress-inducing choices. The bottom line: food not only fuels your mood but can change your mood. One of the quickest and simplest strategies for counteracting stress and eliciting the start of a relaxation response is to engage in the pleasurable act of eating healthy, nutrient-dense foods.

The War on Food

I don't understand why we are always at war with our food. When did food become the enemy? Food is one of the greatest pleasures in life. It's not natural or emotionally satisfying to deny ourselves food to the point of flavorless starvation. This obsession with what we can't or shouldn't eat has led to the forbidden food syndrome. We've suffered through the low-carb diet, denying ourselves bread, potatoes, rice, pasta. Then that was totally reversed, and we rushed to the low-fat diet: no butter, oils, or red meat.

But how many of us succumb to temptation and partake of the forbidden food of the month? And oh, the guilt! We indulge ourselves and feel like sinners. The forbidden food syndrome has condemned us to a sense of weakness and failure whenever we give in, even "just this once," and reach for something on the "don't eat" list.

The irony is that many segments of our population are in fact suffering from obesity. It's alarming to see children, especially, becoming so heavy. As a result, there are many jazzy diets out there, some better than others, promising a cure: Weight Watchers, South Beach, Atkins, Jenny Craig, the Zone, Mediterranean, the Cabbage Soup Diet, the French Let-Them-Eat-Cake Diet, the Blood-Type Diet, the Acid-Alkaline Diet, the God Diet— well, you get the picture. Yet we're still heavier than ever! Why? Is it the sweet sodas, the fast foods, the huge portions? Or is there one central theme: stress? Have you noticed that both stress and obesity are increasing at an alarming rate? What about thin stressed-out women, you might ask? Did you know that it is possible to be a "fat" skinny woman who eats mostly sugary food and has unhealthy fat deposits over her internal organs along with an overwhelmed immune system?

Not all of us need to lose weight. Many of us are thin enough. It's more about eating junk: processed foods with trans fats, a high sugar content, and artificial ingredients. Stress makes us eat more junk food to calm down quickly. Stressed out? Have an éclair, and you feel better immediately, at least for ten minutes. Is it any wonder that when we eat more nutrient-deficient foods, we continue to feel stressed after the effect wears off?

The Low-Fad Diet

It's time to think about a low-fad diet. This diet consists of making a commitment to sustained success and listening to the voice of reason telling us that there is no such thing as a quick fix. Here are some questions to help you alter the mind-set that is impeding you from reaching your goals for healthy eating.

- Do you sabotage your health by eating foods that you know are harmful? Solution: be as loving and loyal to yourself as you would be to others.

Tips for Curing Stress Addiction
Being Overweight Is Linked to Depression

Depression and obesity most likely fuel one another. Women ages forty to sixty involved in a study by Dr. Gregory Simon demonstrated a striking association between weight gain and depression. When women gain weight, they become depressed, and when they are depressed, they have a hard time losing weight. One of the reasons is a loss of self-esteem, as society places a premium on the svelte female form. Keep in mind that men are not stigmatized for being overweight as women are. They do not suffer about their fading looks as women do. Dr. Simon emphasizes that overweight women are not clueless about weight loss; rather, they feel hopeless. The cure lies in strengthening the spirit and finding ways to bolster self-esteem.

- Do you eat to fill an empty, lonely heart? Solution: express your gratitude and appreciation to others and so to yourself. When you appreciate yourself, you take care of yourself.

- Do you eat when you are nervous and pressured? Solution: don't expect comfort food to go the distance the way long-term self-care will. If your weight and activity levels are out of balance, you will not be happy.

- Are your portions too big? Solution: conduct your meals the way you conduct your business. Don't grab more than a fair share.

- Do you replay worries and perceived insults, or do you let them go? When people criticize you, does it trigger eating sugary-fat or salty-fat comfort food? Solution: we all have negative and good voices in

our head. Recognize these negative thoughts and
don't go there. Nip them in the bud. Imagine going
to the fruit store and sorting out the bad fruit from
the good fruit. You have the ability to do it!

You already know that true beauty is not only on the surface;
rather it is the vitality you activate in mind and body, which then
radiates outward. Take the pressure off the obsessive quest for
physical attractiveness. You will feel lighter! When you ease up
on unrealistic images, you can sustain your effort to manage small
goals of achieving a healthy weight and level of fitness.

Avoid extreme measures. Eating only citrus fruits and drinking water (a popular cleansing diet) is not going to work for most
of us, but studies show that cutting out sweetened colas (which
also raise your blood pressure) can make a huge impact. Perhaps
a 10K run is overwhelming, but a thirty-minute walk isn't!

Sticking to the Positive

I have seen it countless times. Positivism and good self-esteem
facilitate weight loss, whereas stress hormones, such as cortisol,
add the pounds or make losing weight difficult.

I have seen women shed pounds consistently when they
shifted their emphasis to the positive. In fact, it worked for me.

After I gave birth to my daughter, Amanda, I had fifteen extra
pounds to lose. Being thin with a petite bone structure, I looked
and felt heavy with those fifteen pounds. So I drank one of those
popular weight-loss mixtures, reputed to stave off hunger for up
to four hours. But five minutes later I said to myself, "Well, what's
for lunch?"

So I gave that diet up the first day. Although I exercised daily,
the weight still wasn't coming off. Finally I decided to accept
myself and see myself as beautiful in my new, full-figured body. I
did what any woman who made such a declaration would do:
I went shopping for a new wardrobe. Returning to work wearing

Tips for Curing Stress Addiction
Lose Weight While You Sleep

Did you know that we produce a weight-loss hormone while we sleep?

When you sleep through the night, your fat cells secrete a hormonal appetite suppressant called leptin, which also triggers the metabolism to burn more calories. Exactly how and why leptin works is still not clearly understood by scientists. Research also shows that sleep helps you deal with daytime stress to both mind and body.

Sleep deprivation threatens the health of fifty to seventy million Americans, according to the Institute of Medicine. Our daytime stress invades our nights, perpetuating the stress-addiction cycle. You cannot deal with your day if you are not getting quality sleep. You need between seven to nine hours of quality sleep to function. Research indicates that losing as little as one-and-a-half hours of sleep for just one night reduces daytime alertness by about a third. Memory and the abilities to think and process information are impaired. Sleep deprivation makes us prone to mood changes, attention deficit, slower reaction times, and accidents, especially when driving. Your health is also impaired. Don't bother counting sheep—it's boring and doesn't work. Here are some tips for the sleep deprived:

- Allocate twenty minutes of worry time earlier in the evening to objectify your problem and consider a solution. Pen and paper work well here. In this way, worrying becomes a defined activity with an end to it.

- Eliminate the work station in your bedroom.

- Create continuity. Go to sleep at the same time every night and wake up at the same time every morning.

- Have sex. No kidding. It works!

- Create personal bedtime rituals: a bath with aromatic fragrances, moisturizing lotion, listening to soft music, visualization. Avoid the late-night news (usually upsetting), surfing the Net, or reading an exciting book (boring is fine).

- Try your grandmother's remedy, warm milk and crackers—they work too! So do bananas, yogurt, figs, and turkey. Avoid sugar, spinach, eggplant, tomatoes, alcohol, and, of course, caffeine. Some of us should not have coffee past noon.

- Exercise large muscle groups in the daytime. Try stretching exercises before bedtime, as these are relaxing.

- Cool down the room and lower the shades. Make sure the room is dark and does not let in the early morning sun. Get in the bed and warm up by cuddling.

If none of these suggestions work, try this trick: force yourself to stay awake. Go to the living room, read a book, pay the bills, and stay up. This will take the pressure off falling asleep.

stylish clothes, I felt attractive and accomplished. After all, I had just created a new life.

Nine months later, the weight just melted off—an interesting parallel, as it took nine months to gain the weight. During those nine months postpartum, I ate healthy foods, did not go hungry, and kept exercising for thirty minutes a day. Most important, I made peace with myself as a larger, more substantial woman. I counted my blessings.

Food Choices and Eating Habits

Take a moment to reflect on your usual food choices and eating habits:

- What are your favorite foods? How do you feel after you eat them?

- Are you a nibbler or a devourer?

- Do you skip meals? Are you a grazer or a three-meal-a-day person?

- What foods do you eat socially? Do you eat differently if you are nervous about fitting in?

- Do you have digestion issues? If you do, after eating what specific foods?

It's good to know what you like to eat. Understanding why you like certain foods and how they make you feel creates real empowerment. How you prioritize your food might provide clues as to how you prioritize your life.

When your life journey takes you through different stages—leaving home for the first time, getting a job, getting married, raising children, experiencing loss—your food preferences can also change! By noticing the transformation from one stage to the next, you may be able to see the correlation between your eating habits and your situation.

Tips for Curing Stress Addiction
The Calorie-Laden Holiday Party

Many of the participants in my workshops are following healthy meal plans, either for weight loss or longevity. However, most feel threatened during ritual family dinners and office parties from Thanksgiving to New Year's, where fatty, sugary foods are either placed on their plates or spread out in gluttonous buffet style. If temptation weren't enough, commands are also issued: "I cooked all day for you. Aren't you going to give your old mother some pleasure?" or "The green apple martinis are divine; let me get one for you." It's hard to say no to your supervisor's tempting suggestion; meanwhile, the pigs in a blanket are coming your way on a silver tray. So, out of that old knee-jerk people-pleasing impulse, not to mention your own self-deception, you eat the artery-clogging, calorie-laden food. Then you feel terrible because this was a case of self-sabotage.

Here's an effective counter from a healthy narcissist: "No, thank you. I appreciate your effort, and I enjoy the visual delight. Everything smells wonderful. But this is not on my diet plan. Please pass the salad." Don't forget, you can bring something healthy to the party and share it with everyone else. "Try my dish. You'll love it." And keep in mind: do not loosen your belt, as you want to sense feeling full; act like Miss Congeniality to keep yourself distracted; and position yourself next to the healthy eaters. If all this doesn't work, then take a long walk afterwards to undo the damage.

By taking a few moments to think about your eating habits, you can also begin to understand your motivation to eat particular foods or to eat at particular times. When do you eat because you feel truly hungry or feel empty, and when do you eat solely for comfort? A satisfying relationship with yourself might be what you really crave, not sugar or fatty processed foods that you use as *heart* substitutes. The cumulative effect of frequently giving yourself credit for meeting any of your goals, no matter how

TALES OF STRESS ADDICTION
Midnight Bingeing

Sara hardly eats anything during the day. No breakfast. At work, she frequently drinks hot water with lemon or chamomile tea. For lunch a little salad. Dinner with her husband is light fare, fish and vegetables with a glass of wine. You would think Sara weighed next to nothing. Wrong! Sara is overweight. She cannot stop bingeing at midnight. Every night, she wakes up at the same time and eats a few chocolate bars, some cake or cookies. "I'm stressed about work. I have to make the right money management decisions for my clients. I replay the day in my head and strategize for the next day." The problem is that Sara's restrictive daytime eating exacerbates her stress, which wakes her up to seek comfort in sugar and fat. Because Sara's sleep is compromised, she wakes up anxious every morning. If Sara ate small, balanced, healthy meals every two to three hours, she wouldn't wake up in the middle of the night to feed her ego, which needs to be bolstered as she is second-guessing her financial decisions and worried about her ranking.

small, fills you up and inspires you in other aspects of your life, especially to succeed in adhering to a nutritious diet.

Also, while you are reconsidering your relationship to food, you might want to try adding some new dishes and spices to your life. Date your diet as if it were a boyfriend to find out what you like and don't like.

Timing and Comfort Food

Timing has a lot to do with serotonin levels. Have you ever craved some chocolate or other sweets or carbohydrates in the afternoon (usually around three) especially in winter, or at night? Here's the reason: in the late afternoon and evenings, when both the amount of sunlight and your own natural serotonin production start to drop, your body craves certain foods to increase its level of serotonin.

However, without enough calcium, magnesium, vitamin D, and B vitamins, your body cannot make serotonin consistently. Eating junk food and fast food, you deprive yourself of vitamins and minerals you need for serotonin production for the long run.

Be aware that following low-calorie diets and skipping meals reduce serotonin supplies quickly, which puts you in a bad mood. To keep your mood up, Susan Kleiner and Bob Condor, authors of The Good Mood Diet, advise eating every two to three hours and getting plenty of sunlight. The body converts sunlight to vitamin D, which increases serotonin levels.

During winter, when there is less daylight in many northern regions, some people become depressed, suffering from a condition known as seasonal affective disorder. This lack of sunlight is likely one of the contributing factors to winter weight gain. Please note that exercise raises serotonin levels to alleviate depression when you don't get enough sunlight. Also, you can get a special light box (consult your doctor on its use) to help compensate for the absence of sunlight.

Tips for Curing Stress Addiction
How to Eat More Frequently

Most women complain that they don't have the time or opportunity to eat. "I'm at work. How do you expect me to eat all
day?" or "Driving the kids around from place to place, doing all
my errands, what do you expect me to eat?" All it takes is a little planning. I don't expect you to munch on a turkey leg. You
can keep some raw almonds, walnuts (not the ones roasted in
oil or salted), dried fruit, an apple, a banana, a high-fiber and
high-protein energy bar in your bag or in your desk drawer. Take
a packet of instant oatmeal to work and mix it with hot water.
You pack the kids' snacks. Now pack your own.

Raising Your Serotonin Level

Women on low-carbohydrate meal plans don't usually last long
on these diets because women, more than men, need carbohydrates to generate serotonin. That's why when you sit down with
a container of rich, creamy ice cream to fill your empty heart,
you feel better, at least for a few minutes.

However, when you observe yourself reaching for these foods,
stop and think! Sugar cravings are self-perpetuating: you will need
more sugar to give yourself that high. Then the guilt will set in,
and you will feel bad about yourself for eating the wrong foods,
which will further lower your self-esteem. Clearly you are needing a serotonin boost, but you can get it without the unhealthy
calories and without perpetuating the stress cycle. Many carbohydrate foods contain the amino acid tryptophan, which the
brain uses to produce serotonin. Consider eating a portion of
whole grains, complex carbohydrates, for a quick pick-me-up. For
example, try any one of the following: a couple of multigrain
crackers (without the trans fats); a portion of oatmeal, brown
rice, or couscous; or a slice of whole wheat toast. One of my

favorite "happy meals" is a slice of whole wheat toast smeared with natural peanut butter. I am getting not only a serotonin boost from the complex carbohydrate but also a quality protein along with healthy fat to stave off hunger. Also, bread with peanut butter evokes a comforting childhood memory.

Such a boost of serotonin doesn't have to come only from food. We'll look at exercise in the second part of the chapter. But there are other simple and effective measures, such as listening to music, that can definitely be uplifting. And don't ignore the power of touch. For example, researchers led by Dr. James Coan at the University of Virginia have shown that holding a spouse's hand when a woman feels stressed restores calmness. Most likely, when you reach for that piece of cake or chocolate candy bar, you are craving love or support. Your

Tips for Curing Stress Addiction
How to Get Your Husband to Eat Healthy

When you make up your mind to eat quality foods to optimize your health and mood, will you be cooking differently for your husband, who likes to eat fatty cuisine like cheeseburgers—thus adding yet another chore to your to-do list? To help a spouse adopt a healthier lifestyle, you have to proceed cautiously, sometimes even surreptitiously—the way you do with the kids. For example, incorporate the flavors your spouse likes into more nutritious fare. Meat might be his kind of comfort food. Make a leaner meat sandwich layered with arugula, roasted peppers, onion, and low-fat Swiss cheese on a whole-wheat roll smeared with mustard, with a side order of baked sweet potato fries. "Great sandwich, honey! By the way, what am I eating?" "Oh, just a secret recipe." Everyone in the family—spouse and children—should be on the same meal plan. They will develop a taste for healthy food and reap the benefits.

spouse (assuming that you are in a good marriage) can stave off a trigger for unhealthy eating and work better than any diet, simply by touching your hand affectionately during dinner or giving you a surprise hug from behind. Similarly, being able to talk in an open, honest, and intimate manner with a loved one, family member, or friend can also bring you comfort and raise your serotonin level without food.

A Bite of Food Science

To keep your brain operating at an optimal level, be aware that it alone, on its own, consumes 30 percent of daily calories and needs a minimum of twelve hundred calories a day for good reaction time, concentration, and memory. Small frequent meals are far more effective at supplying the brain with a steady amount of glucose than three meals a day. Many exercise physiologists suggest eating every two to three hours to speed up metabolism and keep it running efficiently, thereby preventing that big meal sluggishness or that eat-everything-in-sight uncontrollable hunger.

Two-thirds of the brain is composed of fatty acids, which form the synapses, the nerve cell membranes that are responsible for communication within the brain and the rest of the body. Think about the impact of good fat versus bad fat on your brain cells by visualizing the following imagery: if you eat large amounts of saturated fats (fats that are solid at room temperature), such as butter and red meat, your brain cells will take on their rigidity. If, in contrast, you eat monounsaturated fat as found in olive oil and omega-3 fatty acids as found in salmon, your brain cells will be more fluid and flexible; better communication between cells means clearer thinking.

Many studies assert a link between low levels of omega-3 fatty acids and depression. Omega-3s are found in salmon, tuna, herring, mackerel, trout, sardines, and, if you hate fish, walnuts, omega-3 eggs, and flaxseed oil or ground flaxseeds. The fewer omega-3 reserves we have, the more severe the symptoms of depression. Many people who fear eating fish because of mercury, dioxin, and other carcinogens can take fish oil capsules (always consult your doctor, especially if you are taking an aspirin a day or blood thinners). However, eating a varied diet of fish and avoiding tile fish, swordfish, shark, and king mackerel have proven to be fine.

Grandma was right: fish is brain food. Further, what's good for the brain is also good for the cardiovascular system, as heart smart and brain smart are related. So by eating more fish, you will feel more alert and intelligent while preventing cardiovascular disease and arteriosclerosis, which can lead to strokes and dementia. By the way, frying fish is not a good idea, as it cancels out many of the benefits!

Tips for Curing Stress Addiction
How Food Sequence Makes a Difference

Did you know that the order in which you eat your food affects your mental state and has relevance to stress? According to Dr. Judith Wurtman, a researcher at M.I.T and director of Harvard University's TRIAD Weight Management Center, food sequence makes a powerful difference. For example, if you need to be mentally sharp, pile on the protein first. If you need to cheer up, load up on complex carbohydrates first. For example, suppose you wake up feeling a bit weepy, or on edge, ready to pounce. Try a bowl of oatmeal or two slices of whole wheat toast. Thirty minutes later, have your protein, whether it's eggs or yogurt. Or if you have to do a presentation at work or take an exam at school, and need to be sharp, eat a breakfast that emphasizes protein: eggs, breakfast meat, cheese, or yogurt. A short while later, eat your complex carbohydrates.

Superfoods or Superhype?

Superfoods? That's just sensationalism and fad eating. Eat a variety of fruits and vegetables—each is a superstar in its own right, providing you with different nutrients to help you function better and even repair cellular damage. When you go to the supermarket, think in terms of healthy optimism: look for a rainbow array of fruits and vegetables.

Instead of being impressed (and probably overwhelmed) with terms like lutein, lycopenes, flavanoids, sulforaphane, indoles, reseveratrol, and anthocyanins, and driving yourself crazy searching for fruits and vegetables that specifically contain them, simply think in living color, which will generally fulfill your body's needs. You do not want to categorize your food intake like a clinician and take the joy out of eating. Here are some common foods that promote good health. Let color be your guide. (For those of you who wish to know about the chemicals and their benefits, I have included them too.)

- Red-blue-purple: blueberries, blackberries, plums, apples, eggplant, purple cabbage, pomegranate, grapes—anthocyanins, powerful antioxidants, which protect the cardiovascular system and prevent clots

- Red: strawberries, watermelon, radishes, tomatoes, beets, cranberries—lycopenes, which reduce free radical damage

- Green: asparagus, Brussels sprouts, broccoli, green squash, spinach, green cabbage—B vitamins, sulforaphane, and indoles, which are believed to have cancer-fighting properties

- Green-yellow: avocado, honeydew melon, peas, corn—lutein, which prevents macular degeneration

- Orange: sweet potatoes, carrots, apricots, pumpkin, cantaloupe—carotenoids, which repair DNA and supply vitamin A

- Orange-yellow: oranges, mangoes, peaches, pine-apple, papaya—high in vitamin C, which helps prevent and reduce inflammation

- White: onions, garlic—allicin, which has antibacter-ial, antiviral, and antifungal properties

Have fun decorating your plate as a family activity you can do with your children. Enjoy the aftereffects of what you eat; feel what energizes you, makes your immune system vigilant against colds, and doesn't upset your stomach or make you feel nervous. We are all different, so also note if you have any food allergies or intolerances.

The Liquid Diet

Drinking water is high on the list of healthy stress management "activities" because all metabolic processes depend on it. Water helps eliminate many toxins from your body and alleviates fatigue. If you wake up tired in the morning, it is often a sign that you were a little dehydrated overnight. We all know to drink water when it's hot outside, but during the colder seasons we may forget that heating systems dehydrate us too. Depending on activity level and heat, eight to twelve cups of water a day is a good guideline for fluids. Because many of us drink coffee or tea and eat soup and fruits, we can include this additional fluid con-tent as part of the daily eight to twelve cups of water.

Drinking extremely large quantities, however, can be dan-gerous. I know women who drink water all day to suppress their appetite and lose weight. I once saw a female trainer carried out on a stretcher from the gym because she drank water all day with-out eating. Her electrolytes were so low that they were almost nonexistent. And why did a professional who guides other women in nutrition not follow her own advice? She later confided that she was experiencing a lot of stress because her teenage daughter chose to live with her ex. She decided that she needed to lose some weight.

It was commonly believed that coffee raised blood pressure and should be avoided. However, some recent research shows that regular coffee drinkers do not get a spike in their blood pressure. And women (not men) who drink coffee apparently get a memory boost. Coffee apparently is high in antioxidants, and for many people the brew is beneficial in alleviating headaches and promoting alertness. Some researchers claim that coffee drinkers are less likely to get gallstones, Parkinson's, type 2 diabetes, and colon cancer. But we can't forget the importance of moderation and balance: we all know how jittery, speedy, and stressed-out too much coffee can make us feel.

Green tea is made from unfermented leaves and reportedly contains a high concentration of powerful antioxidants called polyphenols, which are touted as potent anti-inflammatory chemicals. In test tubes, green tea has shrunk malignant tumors. Dermatologists claim that green tea can help repair sun damage. For many of us who have fond memories of tea parties when we were little girls, tea has the benefit of a relaxation response cue in addition to its innate relaxing properties, especially herbal teas like chamomile. Hot or cold, tea should be sipped, not gulped, and it's a great way to slow down women on the run.

Soul Food

I am happy to let everyone know that research lauds a piece of delicious dark chocolate, not only as a great mood elevator (which you and I knew all along without the studies) but also as beneficial in relaxing blood vessels and preventing plaque from adhering to arteries—good for both heart and brain.

However, this is not a license to fill up on dark chocolate. Just a small amount of bittersweet chocolate does the trick. More good news, now that over-the-counter cough medicines have been implicated as doing little for a cough except giving you some alcohol to quiet down: hot chocolate has been shown to be much more effective!

Food Aromatherapy

When you are in a negative frame of mind, change your stress level with the odors of food. Dr. Alan Hirsch, director of the Smell and Taste Treatment Center in Chicago, says that food odors have a powerful effect on mood (and they have no calories!). Our sense of smell is the only sense with a direct link to the limbic brain, the old reptilian seat of emotions and basic instincts, like the fight-or-flight response and reproduction.

For example, food odors affect the arousal centers in the brain. Men and women often go out to dinner and then later enjoy themselves sexually. Now you can set this up more scientifically. The male brain especially responds with happy, romantic thoughts when getting a whiff of pumpkin pie, cinnamon, and lavender—combined. Dr. Hirsch says these odors are more effective than the expensive perfume women wear. Duke University's Marian Butterfeld, MD, agrees with Dr. Hirsch's research finding that if you dab a bit of grapefruit juice, or a perfume that smells like grapefruit, behind the ears you will appear on average six years younger to a man! This may be due to his arousal (when he is aroused you look better to him) or to a nostalgic memory, or it may be that the scent of grapefruit is a stress buster.

For women it's the smell of Good & Plenty candy and cucumbers (I'm not making this up), but the arousal is not as powerful as the effect of food odor on men. In any case, these smells are pleasant and evoke a positive, relaxed mood, which is a precursor to arousal.

How Exercise Alleviates Stress Addiction

Research studies over the past fifty years have shown that exercise boosts mood and promotes longevity. One extensive Finnish study concludes that movement is more important to overall health than how much you weigh. Exercise empowers the self, physically and mentally awakening your potential to grow and move forward in life.

Move the Body, and the Mind Will Follow

I've seen women who felt stuck in their jobs and marriages begin a strength training program—lifting weights and doing squats, lunges, and push-ups for thirty minutes twice weekly. Within a year, they were able to move forward in both situations to find greater fulfillment. In fact, they didn't leave their jobs or marriages; they made them work because they experienced greater confidence and self-esteem, becoming more assertive as they worked on improving their intellectual and emotional skills.

As we put on more muscle and increase bone density, learn to coordinate our movements rhythmically, and improve our balance, we transfer these abilities to all the activities of daily living.

Exercising regularly gives you a natural high. You can look down at your relatively smaller problems to see the total picture—then find the solution. Exercise rewires the brain. Stuck in negative mind-sets of hurt, anger, failure, or worry? Don't take my word for it—try a bout of exercise to disrupt these thoughts and restore a sense of control. The great thing about exercise is that it not only releases the negative energy of a specific episode of sadness and frustration but also can prevent new episodes—if you are consistent in continuing your workouts.

By the way, exercise makes you smarter. It's even more effective than doing crossword puzzles, especially when you vary your

TALES OF STRESS ADDICTION

Caregiver, Care for Thyself

A few years ago, my daily schedule ran like this: prepare the children for school; go to work; visit my mother in the nursing home; return home to cook dinner, help with homework, and interact with my husband. But by the time I got home every day, I felt tired and sad. So I decided to shift my exercise time to when I needed it most—between my visit to the nursing home and returning to my home. Each morning, I threw gym clothes and a pair of sneakers in the trunk, worked all day, advocated for my mother, then ran off to the gym. I'd arrive home a new person—bright and cheerful—the real Debbie. What a difference an hour makes! I sweated out my problems and stopped feeling sorry for myself. I realized I could flow with the daily instabilities in my life and find my personal balance. Everyone in my household was the better for my new routine.

workout to challenge your mind, such as by learning new dance steps. Exercise is also recommended for preventing dementia. An Italian study shows that moderate physical activity helps prevent cognitive decline.

You know that stress is not good for the brain. What are you waiting for? Put on your sneakers and walk out the door. You don't have to train as if you were heading for the Olympics; just keep the body moving and have a good, moderate time.

How It Works

According to the American Psychological Association, exercise gives the body a chance to practice dealing with stress and then releasing it. In Step 3, I noted that it is beneficial to challenge yourself in destabilizing mediums (inducing stress) to cultivate your return to homeostasis. In exercise terminology this is known as core training. Also, during aerobic exercise—whether it's running, a step class, kickboxing, calisthenics, tennis, or dancing—you are pushing your body with fight-or-flight stress-response movements. Then when you have finished, you let your body relax and recover, which is the relaxation response. The direct result of exercise is that you become stronger in mind and body, more able to adapt to stressors as you think quickly on your feet.

Similarly, in isometric strength training, you lift weights to increase muscle fibers and build bone density. However, muscle doesn't grow when you stress the body during lifting; it grows during rest. You induce overload (stress), and adaptation follows, and then you repeat the process to advance in strength and spirit—sounds a lot like life. When the amount of weight you are lifting

TALES OF STRESS ADDICTION

Martial Arts for Marital Arts

Many women take a blow to their self-esteem when going through a divorce. Wendy was going through a messy divorce involving police and restraining orders. She was trying valiantly to manage her stress through positive reinterpretation, meditation, and breathing, but I felt she needed something more aggressive to fortify her bruised identity. Wendy chose a martial arts class and began to rediscover her self-confidence. "I found my will again in karate, and I knew I would get over this tough time in my life." After the divorce, Wendy became a black belt. She returned to school and became a nurse practitioner in pediatrics.

becomes easy over time, you go to the next level of intensity and resistance. As you remember from Step 1, acute stress is good for you. Your body working out exemplifies acute stress, which keeps your immune system kicking and your mind focused and clear.

Why So Many Excuses?

Many of us seem to have trouble sticking to a regular exercise regime, reciting the usual range of excuses: "I'm busy," "I'm tired," "There's no time," "They're too sexy in the gym and will judge me."

Many of us resist this healthy method of stress reduction because it requires that we love and care for ourselves—an attitude we have trouble sustaining.

Another underlying issue is that we imagine countless hours of torturous exercise, perceiving it as punishment instead of as a life-affirming activity. However, you don't need a large block of time to exercise, and it's not supposed to hurt. Change your attitude from "Ick, I have to go exercise" to "I can't wait to experience that joyful feeling in my body." Sounds like sex—well, yes, and you'll learn in Step 6 that exercise leads to great sex. Also make sure you like your new workout clothes; you'll be more motivated to use them.

Short-Take Exercising

Exercise generally reduces stress within fifteen minutes, and the health effects last throughout the day. You can calibrate your exercise duration and intensity to match your stress level. If you have more stress, you can exercise a little longer or more intensely.

For example, if you are truly furious or distraught, an eight-minute slow-paced walk won't do it for you. Instead you might need a forty-five minute aerobics class or strenuous walk to cultivate a relaxation response. Find a workout that you will enjoy and that will fit your personality and schedule.

If your schedule makes it difficult for you to work out for thirty continuous minutes, the good news is that you can work out three times a day with ten minutes or so per session, for short bursts of feel-good hormones. Exercise with fast, upbeat music for greater de-stressing synergy. In fact, ten minutes here and there throughout the day has been demonstrated to have a cumulative effect. Also, when you exercise in small spurts throughout the day, you are lowering your blood pressure, restoring focus, and energizing yourself—frequently, as your stressors arise. Aim for regularity: schedule it and just do it. Whatever time you allocate for your workout, if you do less than you intended, don't beat yourself up about it. Like a healthy narcissist, say to yourself, "Great, at least I got to do some of my workout today—better than nothing."

Tips for Curing Stress Addiction

The Benefits of Exercise

- Reduced risk of heart disease and better heart function
- Improved blood pressure control
- Improved cholesterol and triglyceride levels
- Reduced risk of osteoporosis and part of the treatment
- Reduced risk of type 2 diabetes and part of the treatment
- Reduced risk of cancer
- Increased muscle mass
- Improved sleep
- Improved immune system
- Improved brain function
- Improved mood
- Increased stamina
- Enhanced longevity

You Have Options

As in all things, an exercise program should be balanced. Some days you do things to strengthen your body, and other days you do things to strengthen your heart and improve flexibility, alternating cardio days, strength-training days, and stretching days.

Vary your exercise sessions to avoid boredom, muscle overuse, and ultimately burnout. There are so many options for cross-training: aerobics classes, spinning classes, body pump classes, body sculpting classes, personal trainers, machines, trampoline, sports leagues, martial arts, tai chi, Pilates, yoga, dancing, bicycling, swimming, and walking. Let's not forget fusion workouts like Yogalates! Surely there is something for you?

Millions participate in walkathons, marathons, 10Ks, golf games, and tennis matches in the name of charity. Some of us even train for them. For many it is a great social event, and for others it is an opportunity to take the focus off themselves and direct it to their favorite causes. However, remember that charity begins at home: *you* must become your favorite cause.

If you choose to go solo, you can follow videos at home and use dumbbells or household objects, such as detergent bottles (with handles) filled with water (according to your strength), for strength training. You can use your own body for resistance training, doing push-ups off the wall, couch, or counter, or doing triceps dips off the coffee table. While you are watching TV, you

---

 Tips for Curing Stress Addiction
It's a Family Affair

Make exercise a family ritual. Instead of going to a matinee with the kids, try some of these: run relay races, shoot some hoops, dance together, play ball, jog, or bicycle, and of course, you can walk and explore the flora and fauna of your neighborhood.

can exercise during commercials by marching or running in place or doing knee lifts, front kicks, jumping jacks, or abdominal crunches—creating your own version of interval training.

Are you spending a lot of time waiting around in an office or on line at the supermarket getting antsy? Instead of getting stressed, do calf raises or side leg lifts. You can hold a magazine up to your face to appear nonchalant.

Domestic Chores

Did you realize that housework is exercise? If you put your mind into your housework, intending it to be exercise, it gives you an excellent workout combining cardio and strength training. Now that's what I call good multitasking!

For example, when picking stuff up off the floor or emptying clothes into the laundry basket, you should not be hunched over, which could hurt your back. Instead you should be doing a proper squat, which is a total lower-body workout. When you squat, always hold your abdominals in to protect your back, and push off your heels. Now you have added abdominals to your workout by pulling them in toward your back. Vacuuming or mopping the floor is great cardio—put on some music and do it with alacrity—in fact, gyms should offer women and men vacuuming and cleaning mirrors sessions for a great workout. Chopping vegetables and wiping counters and mirrors are great for arms and shoulders. Do a few push-ups off the kitchen counter, and you have worked your upper body.

I love gardening, and tending to my garden can be better for strength training and more aerobic than working out at the gym. And because I enjoy it, I lose track of time, something gym members might envy. In my research, I have found that gardeners are not likely to get osteoporosis. And when I look around at the beauty of nature, I'm filled with serenity. Gardening is my idea of a moving meditation. Don't have a garden? Try indoor gardening or your community gardening association.

Tips for Curing Stress Addiction
Exercise Your Mind

Scientists have been finding more evidence that the human brain is capable of renewing itself and that exercise accelerates the process. Neuroscientist Fred Gage from Columbia University explains, "We've always known that our brains control our behavior, but not that our behavior could control and change the structure of our brains." MRIs show that during exercise, blood flows at a much higher volume to a part of the brain (the hippocampus) responsible for neurogenesis, growth of new brain cells. And if you think that exercise makes the aging brain smarter, imagine your children. University of Illinois scientists studied school-age children and found that those who have a higher level of aerobic fitness processed information more efficiently and were quicker on a battery of computerized flashcard tests. The researchers also found that higher levels of aerobic fitness corresponded to better standardized test scores among a set of Illinois public school students. One theory to explain the growth of brain cells is that exercise speeds the brain's production of serotonin, which could in turn prompt new neurons to grow. One thing for sure, chronic stress damages the brain. Worthy to note: once they had assessed the results of the study, all the neurologists involved committed themselves to vigorous exercise!

Psychological Fitness

Fitness starts in the head as a "conscious workout." Do not talk on your cell phone while you work out; instead, put your mind into your muscle. This will enable you to transfer the benefits of your workout skills—inner focus, awareness of your surroundings, and neurological communication—into other aspects of your daily life. You will be more conscious of exercising control and assuming responsibility while you live in the undiluted present.

Mind Your Muscle

You put your mind into your muscle, not only to execute moves properly so as to reap the benefits of strength and flexibility but also to avoid hurting yourself. Taking the focus off your body during exercise can lead to injuries as you trip during a step class or lift a heavy weight while you are out of alignment.

Working out is an example of healthy narcissism, not because you are looking in the mirror to check out your form while you exercise, but because you are totally into your self, what your amazing body can do with its coordinated movements. You draw evidence from your concrete accomplishments to trust in your ability and intuition.

Another perk: exercise compels you to think about organizing your day around good health. After a hard workout, you are more likely to choose healthy foods instead of a candy bar, because you don't want to cancel out the health benefit of exercise with unhealthy eating. As our body grows stronger, so does our mind. As our mind grows stronger, so does our ability to ward off illness because we do not inflame ourselves with stress.

Fitness improves your activities of daily living, making you more efficient in completing your tasks. For example, if you take your lunch hour at work and split it in two, half for eating and half for exercise or a brisk walk, you will avoid the afternoon

Tips for Curing Stress Addiction
How to Do a Squat and Push-Up for
Total Body Fitness

For a complete lower-body workout using your legs and butt, here's how to do a proper **squat:** pretend that you are sitting on an imaginary chair and keep your heels on the floor. Point your toes out and push off from your heels, driving your power straight up to rise to your beginning standing position while you hold your abdominals in tightly. The lower you squat, the more you tighten up your glutes. Do not hold your breath. Exhale on the exertion phase of the exercise. Aim for a set of eight to twelve repetitions. When this feels comfortable, increase the number of repetitions.

To do a **push-up,** first use your kitchen counter or a sofa with one end tight against the wall, so that it doesn't slide. Place your hands firmly on the counter or sofa and extend your body full length with your weight on your toes. Keep your abdominals tight, your back straight, and your hands directly under your shoulders with fingers facing forward. Lower your chest to the counter or the couch by bending the elbows, keeping them pointing back. Look straight ahead for good alignment. Then push back up with a slow, controlled movement. Don't snap or lock your elbows. Don't hold your breath. Exhale on the exertion phase of the exercise. Try a few, gradually increasing the number of repetitions. When you are finished, stand up tall with your chest open and shoulders back and down, proud of your accomplishment.

slump. Research shows that your more sedentary coworkers will become sleepy and irritable, and will complain more about work and take more sick days. Have you noticed that many companies have a gym on site, or pay for employee gym memberships? Management knows how stressful work can be and that sitting at a computer for countless hours erodes you mentally and physically. This is why they want you to reboot your system with any form of exercise.

Don't Be Afraid of Weight Training

Many women imagine they will bulk up with weight lifting and look unattractive—a female face on a steroidal, masculine body. You need a whole lot of extra testosterone for that, ladies; estrogen is not a muscle-building hormone. You will not bulk up, but you will get stronger and develop harder muscles than you have now. More women than men are at risk for osteoporosis, so lifting weights is a prescription for good health, as it is both preventive and curative. Also, as we age (from the thirties on) we lose muscle mass, and strength training is the fountain of youth for toned muscles. Baby boomers should gear their exercise program toward strength training for both these reasons.

When you strength-train, you isolate the muscle you are working, thinking about contracting it and then fully extending it in a slow, controlled manner without relying on momentum, sending your breath to the area as you exhale on exertion. Studies show that when you focus on the muscle you're working, it grows stronger simply by virtue of the mental component. Strength training not only tones the body but tightens the loose, distracted mind of the stress addict. And the great thing about weight training is that you can quantify your progress objectively by changing up the weights, gradually increasing first the number of repetitions and then the amount of weight.

■ ■ ■

Eating and exercising mindfully will help eliminate stress addiction and help you feel more in charge of your life. Now that you are spiraling upward, stronger and better than before, let's jump-start your inner treadmill, your sense of humor, and have some fun in the next chapter. You can be antic, poetry in motion!

STEP 5

Cultivate Your Sense of Fun and Humor

S tep 5 will show you how to transform electric, nerve-rattling stress into flowing, vital energy. It's time to get healthy, tease out your sense of fun, cultivate a comic eye for life's obstacles, and start coloring outside the lines.

When it concerns your personal joy, you don't have to wait for external events—Jupiter aligning with Mars, a promotion at work, your daughter's going to Harvard, or anything like that—to get happy. You can be joyous for no reason at all, with a happiness and sense of humor that comes from within.

The Importance of Humor

Humor is an amazing and highly effective way to reduce stress and break away from negative experiences with others.

In all of my trainings and workshops I show people how to experience **F–U–N**: Feeling Uninhibited Naturally.

Tragedy or Comedy? You Pick Your Life's Script

The classic plot structure in the theatre is basically the same for a tragedy or comedy—from Shakespeare to Neil Simon. The main character has a big problem, and in the end the problem is solved one way or another. The only difference lies in the perception and framing of this problem, and the point of view; these determine whether there is a sad ending or a happy one.

So goes life. We can plan the most elaborately romantic evening on a moonlit beach and have it end in a miserable argument, or we can clean the kitchen stove together, laughing and really talking it up in a loving flirtation with our spouse. It's not what you do, but how you do it!

Often we intensify an abrupt, thoughtless remark made by our boss or our child into a full-blown crisis, losing our emotional balance as we plot our retaliatory response, unable to think about anything else. However, what if we reduced the comment by putting a comic spin on it so that we can laugh and let it go? How many futile dialogues of repetitive arguments, particularly with teenagers, would be avoided, freeing our energy for more joyous activities? For example, a few years ago I was driving my daughter, Amanda, twelve years old at the time, home from school. "Mom, I would like to buy some eye shadow, eye liner, mascara, and lipstick—you know, makeup—to wear to school from now on." When I explained that wearing makeup to school was inappropriate at her age, she countered with the standard argument that all the girls were wearing makeup and their mothers had no problem with it. Calmly, I stood my ground. Amanda snarled, "Everyone thinks you are so sweet and nice, a real Miss Sunshine, but I know the real you!" Instead of losing it, I replied, "Good—you should know the real me," as I burst into laughter. Amanda, who pretended to cry crocodile tears, could no longer contain her laughter. "Do you want to watch *Gilmore Girls* together?" I asked. "Sure, Mom."

Throw Away the Broken Eggs

Have you grown up hearing this motherly advice: "If life gives you lemons, make lemonade" or "If you break the dozen eggs you just bought, bake a cake"? This may sound practical, but it doesn't sound like much fun (and I'm not saying this just because I'm not a great cook). It's more like a recipe for accepting a constrained, unhappy life. Isn't it time to reject the lemons, throw away the broken eggs, and go beyond merely "making do" and "making the best of things"?

Blind adherence to parental or communal values, especially when they make you feel uneasy, eventually inhibits your spontaneity. Here are some conventional beliefs that can keep you from having any fun:

TALES OF STRESS ADDICTION

The Dark Side of Fun: Shopaholism

"Every day I receive at least five different catalogues urging me to shop. I receive coupons from department stores inviting me to participate in special sales as a 'preferred customer.'"

My client Julia confesses that she is ashamed of her many purchases, cutting off the tags and hiding them in her closet under her old clothes. When the credit card bills inevitably arrive, her spouse chides her as if she were a silly girl for spending too much on clothes and accessories, threatening to cancel her credit cards.

"What started out as fun becomes a nightmare jeopardizing our savings." Most shopaholics are women, and the problem is associated with stress addiction. Here's what many women experience:

Emptiness. Shopping fills an emotional longing.

Boredom. You shop to get that surge of excitement.

Deprivation. If you weren't shopping, you would be eating to fill up the hole in your heart.

Low self-esteem. You shop to relieve the compulsion to possess what others have.

Julia learned to control her urge by finding other ways to have fun with her friends, such as by doing lunch, going to the museum, and exercising—basically, staying away from the mall. When she does shop, it is with cash, not credit cards. Aware of her triggers, she immerses herself in a hobby she enjoys, photography. She can always take photos of the things she wishes to buy!

It's too selfish of me to indulge in purposeless fun or in fun that doesn't involve my family.

I have to be working or accomplishing something to be of any value.

I can't relax when I have nothing to do. I get bored.

You always have to come back to reality, so what's the point of fun?

I'm wasting time when I have fun.

Childish or Childlike?

Both therapists and spiritual leaders will tell you that to view your world through the wondrous eyes of your inner child is a blessing. Some of the participants in my workshops, however,

---

 Tips for Curing Stress Addiction
Self-Limiting Beliefs

Many dearly held proverbs and aphorisms are contradictory, which is more noticeable when they're juxtaposed. Reviewing such opposing statements might inspire you to question your sanity for adhering to these self-limiting thoughts. When you take a closer look, you'll definitely smile.

Money talks.	Talk is cheap.
The only constant is change.	The more things change, the more they stay the same.
Absence makes the heart grow fonder.	Out of sight, out of mind.
Two heads are better than one.	If you want something done right, do it yourself.
Clothes make the man.	Don't judge a book by its cover.
Look before you leap.	He who hesitates is lost.
Don't be a quitter.	Quit while you're ahead.

complain that they could not return to that innocent world where they were little barbarians playing in the sandbox and running through the sprinklers. Nowadays, they say going on a roller coaster might nauseate them and make them dizzy.

OK. I can understand that. We're older now, for sure. So our fun may be a little different; besides we know now about the dark side of things. When was the last time someone said to you, "You look so cute with that piece of broccoli stuck between your teeth and some dried mud in your hair?" Once your eyes have been opened, you cannot return to a state of innocence and inexperience.

But you can release that inner girl within. You can experience the *spirit* of childhood, the part of you that doesn't correspond to the chronological age you see reflected in the mirror. This spirit translates as antic energy that is truly in the moment.

The spirit of childhood is all about living simply, like falling in love with an old lamp you find in a flea market or being totally immersed in a game of bridge. Those of us who are able to experience the spirit of childhood don't overanalyze what we like to do or when we like to do it. We try not to worry about what the neighbors will think when we are disheveled or when we express exactly what's on our mind. We let it all hang out, as I did the time I permitted my daughter go to the mall for the first time on her own to meet a friend. Not wanting her to know that I was going to check up on her, I went incognito wearing my husband's olive trench coat, his gray fedora, and a pair of black party glasses. When I was satisfied that all was well, I drove home, the undetected detective. Meanwhile, my husband returned home unexpectedly. Can you imagine the look on his face when he opened the door? "It was a good thing Amanda didn't see you. How would she have introduced you to her friend? This is my mother, Agent 99."

Then just last Monday I decided to pressure-wash the deck in anticipation of spring planting. I looked like the terminator

Tips for Curing Stress Addiction
Formula for Healthy Living

The American Medical Association has officially labeled worka-holism an addiction. In fact, workaholics tend to seek out high-stress jobs to act out their addiction. Also, workaholics are generally suspicious that others will take credit for their work, so they do not like to delegate and are reluctant to take vaca-tions: they might be perceived as dispensable. However, research shows that when you take a vacation from work, even a four-day weekend, you are more productive and creative when you return.

A friend of mine whom I'll call Nora took her BlackBerry into the Amazon rain forest and complained, "I'm not getting any reception here."

Wow. Poor Nora completely overlooked the silence, beauty, and profound peace of the rain forest. Here's a better way to experience such a vacation; it's a formula for balance: *concentrated energy + relaxation = healthy living.*

These two powerful opposites create the life force that helps you grow and advance in spirit. You already know and live the action part of this equation. However, relaxation is of equal, not less, importance. Don't override your rhythm by overload-ing your day with action. Your own heart serves as an excellent example of these two opposites, contracting the muscle during exertion and relaxing between beats. Remember: your heart is designed to last a lifetime—unless you overload it.

with that gizmo slung over my shoulder. I was doing a fairly good job when my husband opened the glass sliding door and told me I had missed a section. He was right, of course; he always is when it comes to spotting a flaw. I smiled and asked him to step outside and show me exactly where. At that moment when he was hunched over the bricks, I quickly disconnected the motor, reattached the spray nozzle to the hose, and let him have it full force. He was dripping, cold, soaked to the skin. "Very funny," he laughed as he grabbed the hose and turned the tide on me. We were quite a sight: two adult kids, laughing, dripping wet, and chilled to the bone, yet so happy.

Fun in our complex, technological, cluttered world means restoring the balance by embracing simplicity: simple living, simple eating, simple heartfelt expressions, and simple goals.

Look back at your old photos, the personal evidence of the good times (for the most part). What past experiences stand out for you in terms of great fun? When you reflect on your favorite photos, are they the ones where you posed all dressed up for an expensive evening of structured fun, or the candid shots of floating on a raft in the pool, trudging in white snow, or baking bread in the kitchen with white flour on your nose? You can bring this understanding of your past identity to who you are today. Perhaps it's time for a "fun makeover," a relaxed renovation of what has turned into a formal or what-is-expected-of you kind of fun.

Do you work long hours from Monday to Friday just to enjoy Sunday (Saturday usually being laundry and household chores day)? Living like this seems out of balance. How can you put some extra fun back into your five-day work week? What can you do each day just for you—a special enjoyable activity to anticipate? Anticipation is at least half the fun.

What Would Lassie Do?

What could be more natural, amusing, and emotionally simple— the antidote to technology—than a pet? Pets are adorable, funny, unconditionally loving stress relievers—unless you are allergic or live in a no-pets-allowed apartment. Stroking a cat or dog lowers blood pressure, puts us in the moment, and releases a relaxation response. You might be surprised to learn that compared with human support, the presence of pets has been proven to produce a greatly reduced stress response—perhaps because pets don't judge. One study found that when the human was experiencing a stressor, pets both diminished the perception of stress and served as a buffer. Pets also remind you to get in touch with your own animal nature—no rationalizing or suppression, simply responding to "Do I enjoy this or not?" And once you stop rationalizing and choking emotions down, you are open to a more humorous or playful perception of the little absurdities of daily life.

Getting in touch with your animal nature can simplify a problem that you might tend to magnify with your intellect. When I attended a lecture given to cancer patients by Dr. Bernie Siegel, author of *Love, Medicine and Miracles*, the audience was roaring with his unexpected response when someone in the audience asked him a serious question and he said, "Let's see, what would Lassie do?" Lassie, a great rescuer, is also incredibly funny from another perspective. The writers of the show endowed her with human traits, in keeping with the way many pet owners perceive their own pets.

When I recall as a little girl watching Lassie on TV every Sunday night, I conjure up that highly perceptive and intuitive collie, understanding sophisticated human speech and responding with a couple of loud barks, to which Timmy or Timmy's parents would answer, "Oh, I see, girl. You need us to follow you for a few miles to the abandoned well to rescue the missing little girl who has fallen in and injured her leg." I laugh remembering my own, as well as the TV audience's, naive belief in Lassie's superior wisdom and communication skills.

Then there was that keenly intelligent dolphin, Flipper, who ruled the sea and counseled a coast guardsman and his two sons.

What animal image or scenario puts it all in humorous perspective for you?

Laughter Is Free Medicine

There are five commonplace ways in which we use humor. Which one is your style?

1. I make others laugh in order to be well liked and feel good about myself.
2. I make others laugh to lighten their load and cheer them up.
3. I laugh to generate happiness inside myself when I need a good laugh.
4. I laugh nervously when I feel frustrated or anxious.
5. I like to take a jab at others when I laugh.

Numbers 1, 2, 4, and 5 are attributes of stress addiction. You make light of a "situation" for someone else's benefit or behave in a self-deprecating manner to reduce external validation. Or you might make self-deprecating remarks to solicit external validation for the purpose of self-soothing. You laugh nervously and make sarcastic remarks as symptoms of emotional overload and low self-esteem. You're unable to let go with a rip-roaring belly laugh. However, when you laugh to amuse yourself, as in number 3, you are implementing Norman Cousins's healing strategy, "Laughter Is the Best Medicine."

Laughter has wonderful physiological benefits. Doctors call humor "free medicine," and exercise physiologists call it the "inner treadmill" because it has benefits similar to exercise. Humor strengthens not only our muscles but our brain as well. For example, laughter enhances our problem-solving ability because it helps the brain de-stress and do its work with a clear focus. Laughter also provides pain relief by releasing endorphins, which especially reduce aches and pains that are induced by stress.

TALES OF STRESS ADDICTION
Dark Humor

Laughing during a funeral is generally considered inappropriate: you are grieving for a loss, participating in a formal ritual to begin the process of closure. When my mother passed away, I arranged for a funeral service in an Orthodox Jewish chapel, as per her wishes. At the time, I had been creating workshops for stressed Dominican nuns and had set my cell phone ringtone for their calls to Handel's "Hallelujah Chorus." At my mother's service, I was sitting with my daughter, Amanda, in the mourner's chapel when suddenly my cell phone played Hallelujah loud and clear. This raised a few eyebrows, and my daughter, absolutely horrified, cried out, "Shut the phone, Mom, shut the phone!" My large pocketbook was cluttered (like my state of mind), and it was difficult to find my phone amid all the somber paperwork, so the very Christian Hallelujahs continued to play on. Suddenly, Amanda and I burst into hysterical laughter, as did a few other Hassidic women who passed by; the tears rolled down our faces. We both knew that my mother, who had a generous capacity for humor, would have enjoyed this opportunity to alleviate the sadness.

William James summed it up best: "We don't laugh because we are happy, we are happy because we laugh." You are literally only one belly laugh away from an endorphin rush!

Laughter improves respiration, increases the number of immune cells, relaxes muscles, lowers blood pressure, and decreases the likelihood of a second heart attack. Studies reveal that even *anticipating humor*—such as by going to see a comedy that has received rave reviews or by looking forward to reading the cartoon section of a newspaper or a funny e-mail—jump-starts the immune system and lowers blood pressure. Laughter can activate your instinct to heal yourself. When you are relaxed, you can come up with positive solutions or at least process your grief within the much larger context of your life. The more you practice laughter as a coping mechanism, the more adept you become at reducing the inflammatory response of stress by quickly decompressing. Eventually, a humorous interpretation will become more natural and automatic for you.

Many religions believe that laughter is an expression of a heightened spirituality because the goal of spirituality is joyous appreciation. When you genuinely laugh at other people's witty remarks, you accomplish two things: you help them feel good about themselves and release your own stress: while you "do unto others," you are also helping yourself. It is believed that God helps those who help themselves—what amazing synchrony!

Even if you believe that your childhood made you more serious, or predisposed you to negativity because of poor parenting or poverty, that's no excuse for your mood today! Note that many funny personalities originated from a darker side or a more deprived background—for example, Mark Twain, Oscar Wilde, Woody Allen, Jerry Seinfeld, Larry David, Richard Pryor, John Belushi, and Rosie O'Donnell. Laughter helped them shine and allowed them relief from their anxiety and emotional pain. In fact, some children who have problems at home assert their individuality as well as reject mainstream values by becoming the class clown. Many of them turn the conventional ideas and ordinary disciplines of school inside out and upside down to discover the absurd details many of us don't see at first. This kind of irony, sarcasm, and revelation of the ultimate absurdity of our lives makes us laugh, and it's wonderful!

Humor and Romance

Let's consider the differences between female humor and male humor. Men use humor to tease a lot. It's a way of being critical and displaying their status. Women laugh at men's jokes to show appreciation and be liked (and let's be honest: sometimes men's jokes are funny).

What might be annoying in your relationships at home or at work is that you are expected to laugh at all the men's jokes while they don't appreciate yours. So let us women make it a goal to reverse the roles, to elevate and communicate our own status. When women are producing the humor and men can laugh at women's jokes, there's truly a happy balance and blend. When a man laughs at a woman's jokes, he is showing her respect and acknowledging her status, which is a lot different than his saying, "Please don't ruin the punch line the way you always do" or "Women don't know how to tell jokes!" These comments at her expense build up resentment in the female heart. To sum up, your self-worth rises when he laughs at your witty remarks. It's your turn to be funny!

Humor can play a powerful role in diffusing tension and conflict in our relationships or marriage. People who kid around with their spouses in everyday situations tend to be happier in their marriage than couples who don't, according to relationship expert John Gottman.

Gender Differences in What Makes Us Laugh

Studies reviewed by Robert Provine from the University of Maryland show that gender differences in humor actually begin at an early age.

Among British children viewing cartoons, for example, girls laughed more with boys than with girls, and girls returned boys' laughter more often than boys returned girls' laughter. Apparently laughter is a social lubricant that little girls use to engage little boys. Little girls also appear to try harder with boys than with other girls, whom they don't need to impress. Remember when you were dating—did you a laugh a bit louder and more often at his jokes? Was this one of your techniques to impress him in order to get him to like you more than the other girls?

Researchers at Stanford University reported that women prefer humor that involves narratives, stories, and personal information. Women are also found to be more analytical in their response to jokes, using both their brain hemispheres to process and react to the ideas and information in any funny story.

Women tend to be self-mocking and like to use improvised humor to promote cohesiveness. This makes sense: women are caregivers and nurturers, busy multitaskers, who use this style of humor to cope with the never-ending stream of little emergencies. Research shows that women use self-deprecating humor to lower their blood pressure and release tension. Otherwise, it might be virtually impossible to continue to live this highly demanding lifestyle without paying a steep price in health and happiness. Instead of experiencing an emotional meltdown because you were so overwhelmed with work and taking care of the children that you forgot about dinner in the oven, you announce your reality— "Oh silly me, I burned dinner tonight!"—using a humorous tone to release tension and, most important, to head off any opportunity for someone else to further fan the flames with criticism.

The opposite is true for men. Most men gravitate toward slap-stick Three Stooges–type comedies and one-liners, which are simpler for them to process. They don't like to make fun of themselves. Self-mocking humor lowers their status and reduces their dominance, which makes them more stressed. For men, humor is differentiating and competitive, a way for them to stand out. They enjoy making fun of others to increase their status, especially when competing for a woman's attention. Men like gross humor and telling rehearsed jokes because they're hoping for a guaranteed response that wins our love and respect.

Generally, when women are polled, the majority want to be with "Someone who makes me laugh." However, the majority of men want "Someone who laughs at my jokes." A woman who deploys a typically male sense of humor—one that's aggressive or competitive—is a turnoff to men, says Don Nilsen, a linguistics professor at Arizona State University in Tempe and an expert on humor. Many men feel threatened by a woman with an aggressive wit, perceiving her as a rival or worrying that they'll become a target of her sharp tongue.

"I think every man in the world admires the humor, even the sexual put-down humor, of someone like Joan Rivers," Nilsen says. "But very few men want to marry her."

Knowing about this kind of research gives you the advantage. If you want to get along with the men in your life—your father, husband, brother, colleague, or boss—make him feel better about himself and reduce your personal stress by laughing at his jokes even if they are simple and obvious, with nothing to process.

Why should you laugh at his stupid jokes, especially if you are angry or unhappy with him? Because most men are hardwired to hear a woman's laughter as a sign of personal validation. And once the stress and tension have been defused, you can create a situation where you too can be funny, in your own way. Now you can reframe that negative situation into a funny story or positive family myth. When you laugh at his jokes, he will be eager to please you and laugh at yours.

Nothing gives my husband, Steve, more pleasure than making fun of my sense of direction. "Meet me on the northeast corner" is a recipe for disaster. I don't know why this is so funny; I simply don't have a compass in my head. When I give him directions, he reverses what I say and lets me know that he reversed my lefts and rights, and laughs and laughs. However, when we were in the south of France, hiking in sunflower fields and vineyards, as a gardener I was in my element. I created markers in my head—a rock jutting out in a particular way, a broken picket fence. When it came time to leave, Steve lost his bearings, and we walked in circles. "Well, Mr. Compass-in-Your-Head, lead us out!" And who would believe it: I led us out. "Look, there is the rock, and there is the broken fence." I did a victory dance—after years of being directionally challenged, I could lead us out of any field of flowers. "Okay, so you can find your way out of vineyards. How many vineyards are there in New York City?"

Home Improvement

When little annoyances pile up at home, can you turn them around with a little smile and touch of humor? Here are a few more ideas.

- Your spouse is really annoyed that you are vacuuming loudly during the big game. He shouts over the din of the vacuum cleaner that you are disturbing him, to which you might ordinarily respond that unlike him, sitting with his feet sprawled out on the coffee table, you are cleaning up the mess he made. Instead you suck up the potato chips off his lap and make a lot of extra noise by turning up the machine a notch higher before you shut off the vacuum cleaner and say, "You're right! I think I have been working too hard. I need a break." You communicate your feelings and laugh while you relax and do your own thing.

- Your spouse and children arrive home starving and tired from work and school, but there is no dinner on the table because you have been busy. "Where's dinner?" they growl at you. To which you can say with a big smile on your face, "You didn't pick it up on the way home? Or do you mean to say, 'Can I help you with dinner?' Thank you for offering to help. Please make the salad and set the table." They will begin to realize that dinner is a family affair.

- You call your fifteen-year-old son artistic when he finds matching socks.

- You describe your husband as a good communicator when he answers the phone once in a while.

- You portray your family as athletic when they get up from the table to get their own second helpings.

- Your husband has been working longer hours because he fears slipping from the top of the pyramid. He's been too busy to take most of your phone calls during the day, and when he does respond, he sounds abrupt. The old you might have felt insecure and invalidated. The new you perceives this as an opportunity for fun. Write a funny job resume, listing your traits and experience. Send him an e-mail at work with a cover note: "I want you to get to know me better."

Eventually your spouse and family will imitate your behavior—remember, you are the center of the house and set the mood. Make a competition out of it: Who is the most outrageous, fun-loving person in your home?

Have Fun Playing Your Part

If you want to become powerful and dynamic, a woman on the move toward self-actualization, you have to stop taking yourself so seriously. Anything that takes you away from yourself—such as anger that invades your rhythm, or criticism that hurls you into a negative loop—stops you from seeing the happiness right in front of you. Fresh and unusual expressions, physical and verbal, make you pause with renewed enthusiasm. Fun makes you creative. And there is almost nothing that creativity can't solve!

Build Up Your Funny Bone

For many women, humor does not come naturally as a coping device. Maybe it's because being silly and childish has always been more of a guy thing. We women are supposed to be nurturing, stable, and serious. So for us humor may require planning and dress rehearsals to express what seems like spontaneity. Humor researchers advise us to build up a humor reservoir so that we can turn on the tap when we need it. As you experienced when you began learning to dance or drive, you may feel awkward contributing funny, witty remarks to a conversation, particularly when you are angry, sad, or self-conscious underneath.

Begin by smiling this very minute, even if you believe that you have nothing to smile about. Your smile, even if it is a bit tenuous or awkward, can serve as a cue for your body to start releasing serotonin and stop with all the negativity.

No matter how stressed out, awkward, or annoyed you may feel in the moment, try to use humor to release the tension and find a different point of view toward whatever is going on with you. Think of your favorite comedians and the techniques they use. What about Phyllis Diller and her incredible spirit of irony and survival? Or the absurd silliness of British farce like Monty Python? Or the free-associative, brilliant improvisation of Robin Williams? What a funny trip he leads us on. Or the satire of Jon Stewart or

TALES OF STRESS ADDICTION

Wigging Out

I remember how much fun I had when my girlfriends took me to a cheap wig store on my birthday, and we all bought wigs for about $15 each. I chose a straight, long-haired red wig, my blonde friend chose a curly black wig, and so on. The four of us strolled arm in arm down a busy Manhattan street singing and laughing. We felt as though we had become different people, anonymous and open to wild adventure. We waltzed into an elegant restaurant, where both men and women gaped at us. Men thought we were hookers and smiled wickedly. During the meal, my scalp itched, and upon scratching my head, my wig tilted, causing my dark hair to peep out from under all the red. The wig began feeling heavy, and in the middle of the meal, I just whisked it off! How we all laughed! Soon a number of chic women came over to our table wanting to know where we had purchased our gorgeous wigs. They wanted to buy them too! But it wasn't really the wigs they wanted to buy; it was the capacity for fun that they represented.

By the way, when I returned home, my daughter, Amanda, was just stepping off the school bus. I put my wig back on to have some more fun. She walked right past me. Now that's what I call a transformation!

the bad boys of *Saturday Night Live*—Chris Rock, Adam Sandler, David Spade, and Chris Farley—where nothing is sacred.

Imitate what you like about your favorite comedians. At the very least, you can repeat their jokes, gestures, and comic scenarios, preferably putting your own spin on them. However, humor, whether rehearsed or spontaneous, takes practice, the same kind of practice involved in cultivating a relaxation response. It's something you can do during the good times for use during the bad times.

Try the following suggestions:

- Take a five- to ten-minute humor break each day.

- Read jokes, add to a humor notebook, look at funny photos, or listen to a funny tape.

- Watch TV comedies or DVD comic films for as long as it takes for you to start laughing; then jot down jokes as you hear them. It took one woman in my class eight hours of comedy watching before she started laughing, and then she couldn't stop.

- If you hear a funny joke that you like, practice telling it three times out loud to yourself. You are now ready to remember and share it with others; while you're at it, make a funny face or put your whole body into the telling. Your "audience's" laughter will convince you that you are funny, and you will laugh together.

Then start searching for everyday humor, the absurd, silly, incongruous activities that go on around you each day. Check out the funnies or the *New Yorker*'s cartoons for a visual perspective.

See Your Life as a Sitcom

Humor helps you become more objective about yourself. James Thurber said, "Humor is emotional chaos remembered in tranquility." When you look back at conflicts or problems that might not have been funny while they were taking place, distance allows you to perceive them as though they were happening to someone else, making you more likely to laugh and release the negative emotion. The goal is to bring this kind of objectivity into your daily experiences while they are happening.

Try to see your life as a sitcom, as though you were watching it happen to Lucille Ball or Marie Raymond—surely you would be laughing. Once you are laughing, you substitute pleasure for negativity. This is how it works: you cannot feel angry, depressed, or resentful and laugh at the same time, in the same way that you can't feel nauseated and hungry at the same time.

My life has had its farcical moments, such as my big debut dinner party for friends when I was a newlywed. I was baking stuffed Cornish hens for the main course. "That's strange, Debbie . . . I don't smell anything in the oven!" My friend Susie remarked. I pooh-poohed the criticism. "That's because my oven is super clean." When I checked, though, I realized in horror that I had forgotten to turn on the oven. "Honey, when's dinner?" my husband, Steve, asked. "Tonight we are going to start with the best part of the meal, dessert, and work our way back," I announced a bit nervously.

Wit is a creative process. When you use humor, you develop your mind as you use your imagination to put together the unexpected or insert a surprising comment in a familiar dialogue. One of the biggest problems for stress addicts is dealing with ambiguities and uncontrollable glitches. Cultivating your wit can get you in the habit of expecting the unexpected and acting with good-natured resilience.

Change It Up

Nothing deadens the heart like routine. You lose the present moment in the robotic performance of the same old tasks.

Tips for Curing Stress Addiction
Fun Activities to Change Your Routine

- Become a tourist in your own neighborhood.

- Check out your newspaper for free fun. Libraries have free film festivals. Parks have free concerts and fairs.

- Do volunteer work with friends for a synergistic effect.

- Grab a bottle of wine and go stargazing and moon watching.

- Visit a Porsche or Rolls Royce dealer and test-drive a convertible—a car you might dream about, but can't buy—just to see how it feels.

- Ride your local ferry and have a picnic on board.

- Create a personal retreat at home to call your own. Build it, decorate it, and use your five senses to individualize it. You don't need a lot of space; even a corner will suffice. Make room for what really matters to you.

- Visit a magic store and learn some tricks.

- Take a faux painting or tiling class at Home Depot for a creative project to beautify your space.

- Try a belly dancing class. This dance form has been around for five thousand years, so there must be something to it!

- Create your own signature drink or dessert.

- Sit in a café and watch passersby or those seated near you, the way the French do.

Try this simple experiment: stir your coffee backwards. See how you pause for a brief second or two and imbue the "same old, same old" with a new consciousness? Similarly, take a new route to work to be more alert. In the same spirit, change where you always sit at the kitchen table. See if you don't see things from a slightly different perspective. If you and your spouse always sit in the same chair or on the same spot on the couch to watch TV, switch. Relocate your knickknacks to different places in the house. Doesn't everything appear wonderfully new? I haven't even suggested a fresh coat of paint in a bold new color.

To Thine Own Self Be True

Many stressed-out women are advised to cultivate spirituality and release themselves from mundane desires and tensions by meditating quietly, doing yoga postures, or sitting in a lotus position while chanting in a strange language. For some of you, this might be helpful and pleasurable. For others, this might be stressful and painful, as you might have to compose a shopping list in your head while you meditate just to get through it!

Don't do yoga or meditation because you ought to do it, because the East is in vogue now and you are pressured to be enlightened.

Any form of fun and laughter for its own pleasurable sake will contribute more to your spiritual growth and overall happiness than *pretentious* or *mandatory* contemplation. In fact, some women eager to dive into yoga have been hurt doing some of the postures! Slowly dip your feet in and see if you like the experience.

Don't force yourself to become something you're not, just because it is chic to take the road not taken (predictably unpredictable). Don't use such discipline or enforced exercise as an excuse to avoid or postpone liberating the hidden girl within because you are afraid of what you will find inside yourself.

It might seem like a quick fix in the right direction of self-realization to just take off, chuck it all, and escape. However, remember that stress has kept you running away from yourself all along. Instead, I invite you to soar by experiencing new things within the context of your daily life, the real place where you live with your family and work with your colleagues. Dare to be more spontaneous, to tell people what you really think, to be less accommodating.

It's time to free yourself from that *ought to* voice in your head and have some fun that resonates just for you.

And remember that when it comes to fun, it's not an all-or-nothing proposition. If you planned a day at the beach but the weather didn't cooperate, take the party indoors. Can't take a week off from work? How about a weekend, how about a day? Entertaining and feeling stressed—not a recipe for fun either for you or your guests? Combine prepared store-bought foods with your own cooking, and voilà! You have a semi-homemade meal like the ones Sandra Lee demonstrates making on her cooking show!

Can't your heart sing today? OK, just hum a tune.

The State of Flow

I have saved the best for last. Now that you have learned how to shift gears from anger and frustration to a more peaceful and objective state of mind through humorous reinterpretation, you need to know that getting into a good mood doesn't always require a specific fun activity or belly laugh. It would be ironic if such an approach actually fed the adrenaline junkie living inside you, creating what-do-we-do-next-for-fun pressure or, even worse, a "to-do list for fun" mind-set.

So let's watch out for that potential addiction to sustaining the adrenaline of forced fun. Instead get a sense of your own

TALES OF STRESS ADDICTION

Dancing with the Stars

I literally waited all winter for summer break, so that I could take Clay's Tuesday-morning dance classes in my gym. Clay was a professional choreographer and dancer, and by the end of each ninety-minute session, you felt as if you could perform a routine for Alvin Ailey. I knew beforehand that I would be at a disadvantage, as I was starting in "the middle of the movie." Shyly, I planted myself in the back of the room. What difference that made, I didn't really know, as the room was completely mirrored. Clay, charismatic and the consummate professional, danced into the room as the music boomed. I tried to follow, but was a bit clumsy to say the least. Suddenly, I noticed the video guy—he was taping the class. Everyone knew about this, of course, but me the newbie. I tried to be inconspicuous, but the steps were complicated. When everyone grapevined to the left, I was on the right. Quickly I slid over to their side. Oh no: horror of horrors, the video guy had the camera on me! Perhaps he was planning to turn this into a comedy. At that point I just let it go and gave into the music, doing a little bit of Clay's steps and a little bit of my own choreography. I could certainly try to look the part. I started to have fun and flow with the rhythm, the teacher, and the other dancers. By the end of the class, I was dancing in sync with the others. I thanked Clay for an amazing class, and the video guy remarked, "You're pretty gutsy. Good job."

rhythm. To heal stress addiction, it's important to be quiet with your self and to experience your personal flow, your separateness, as calmly delightful. This means getting comfortable with experiencing things by yourself. Find a place to withdraw from the nervous energy that marches in from people, responsibilities, and distractions, leaving you numb with stress. Instead of thrashing around, get into a state of flow.

To be in a state of flow means to become one with whatever you are doing. Mind and body are in sync, as when a golf swing emanates from the golfer without the mind breaking the swing into a series of prescribed movements. When we don't flow—for example when we first learn to dance—we sacrifice rhythm and style for technique. We concentrate so hard on getting it right that our movements are forced and jerky, and we forget to have fun. But oh, when it all comes together!

Regular practice will promote the flow of self-soothing thoughts. Getting into your own flow is also a great time to practice the breathing exercise you learned in Step 2. Learn to sense your own state of flow, when the internal chaos quiets down and the demand for drama dissipates as your own sweet inner voice lets you know what you need for self-care.

■ ■ ■

As long as you are on a raft swept away by life's current, you might as well get swept away with passion. When you start growing as a unique individual, you blossom. With your quick laughter, sense of fun, and ability to flow, it's time to release your sensuality, as you'll learn in Step 6.

STEP **6**

Jump-Start Your Libido

un breeds fun. Although it's wonderful that you're back in touch with your once hidden spirited girl within, Step 6 will show you how to howl for the wild woman in you to burst out so that you can reclaim your sensuality. As a one-time victim of stress addiction, you may find that sex and sensuality are the most submerged parts of your identity and creativity, so your libido may need a jump-start to get up to speed again.

Life energy and sexual energy are intertwined—you could say joined at the hip. Your sexuality is your passion print, as unique as a fingerprint. I don't care what kind of clothes you wear—revealing blouses or sweats all day—you express your passion print in the way you move; the scent you emit; how you speak with your eyes, part your lips, and breathe. Your sexual life and its fantasies, secret or shared, are also part of your unique passion print.

Obstacles to Sex and Sensuality

Think about desire for a moment and its relationship to stress addiction. If you are depleted by overzealous parenting, work, household responsibilities, an improper diet, a sedentary lifestyle, and poor sleeping habits, you will not feel sexy—plain and simple.

Consider also if your lovemaking has become too goal oriented—focused only on achieving the all-mighty orgasm. You do want to have orgasms, for sure, but you know how much intimacy and long-term tender lovemaking you lose if orgasm becomes the only point of your sex life.

Or maybe you use the incredible busyness caused by stress addiction as an excuse to contain your sexual energy and justify not having sex. Are you angry at him? At yourself? Do you feel anxious about having sex?

One would think that sex, an act that is both physically and emotionally healthy for you *and* pleasurable, would become part of your personal rhythm. Yet you have more excuses for not having sex than you have for avoiding exercise!

I'm too tired.

I have a headache.

I'm stressed out.

I'm mad at you.

I'm grieving.

I look unattractive.

I have too much work on my mind.

I don't have to respond to your biological urges.

I'm not in the mood.

I feel numb from the waist down.

I have PMS.

I'm in menopause.

I could go on, but I don't want to fill up the chapter with phony excuses. Besides, you are probably more complex and inventive in dreaming them up. Instead, I want to persuade you to enjoy regular, enthusiastic sex. When you make a commitment to jump-start your low libido, you will cure stress addiction and reclaim your joy.

Recognizing and Understanding the Problem

If you are experiencing low libido, it is time to *stop* accepting it. It doesn't have to be this way. Don't tell me you are living with your best friend or a roommate, please. Sure, anthropologist Helen Fisher from Rutgers University claims that the love fever of our early-stage relationship has to break like any fever. Her research demonstrates how difficult it is to sustain over time. Accordingly, she says, companionate bonding becomes the most desirable next stage of a successful marriage.

I agree with her up to this point of departure: that although friendship might take center stage after the honeymoon phase of the early years, don't underestimate the supporting role of sex, which fuels that companionship. Don't use this research-based interpretation as an excuse to justify your own relationship stalemate as inevitable. Many stress-addicted, low-libido, or even sexless marriages don't reach the drastic stages of divorce, separation, or desertion because couples stay together despite their unhappiness, suffering from a kind of relationship inertia. In one study, 30 percent of couples admitted to living "wed-locked," or locked into a loveless marriage. A relationship that began with initial passion and optimistic energy for building a life together gets eroded by routine realities. The result: two people living in a non-divorce.

A non-divorce is like being in purgatory or limbo. You and your spouse continue to live in the same home, nodding politely to each other in the hallway and ignoring each other in the bedroom. The two of you go out to dinner with friends; you take family trips together; your money is in a joint account; the children appear to be functioning well. You are just good friends.

I don't know about you, but I have a lot of friends. I want a lover. If my husband is my best friend, this is a bonus; however, the job description calls for a lover.

But settling for being friends doesn't have to be your lot in life. The latest neuroscientific research has sifted the original high of romance into individual fragments of visual, olfactory, tactile, and neurochemical transmitters so as to analyze love. Arthur Aron, a psychologist from the State University of New

TALES OF STRESS ADDICTION

The New Dual Master Bedrooms

The non-divorced but wed-locked syndrome has been picked up by the National Association of Home Builders and Architects, which predicts that 60 percent of custom houses will have dual master bedrooms, his and her wings, by 2015. And this is not just for the rich. What could be called the sleeping-alone-at-home routine is currently available to middle-income homeowners who move into a spare bedroom, the family room, or the den. The most common excuse: Daddy snores too loudly.

York–Stony Brook, has conducted fMRI studies (functional magnetic resonance imaging, a method of observing which areas of the brain are active at any given time) on couples who claim to be romantic after years of being together. To his surprise, they were not exaggerating or imagining things! Their brain scans prove that these couples are still having the same neurological reactions that couples have in the early stages of their sexual honeymoons. I want you and your beloved to be one of those couples. We know it's possible.

So begin by making an appointment to see your doctor and ask her to evaluate if the source of your low libido is a hormonal imbalance or an underlying illness like diabetes, cardiovascular disease, thyroid malfunction, anemia, or an autoimmune disease. A waning libido can also be a symptom of depression. Note that a number of antidepressants, such as Paxil, Zoloft, and Prozac, cause low libido, whereas others (for example, Wellbutrin) do not. Discuss treatment options and the side effects of medications with your doctor.

Tips for Curing Stress Addiction
It's in His Kiss

After a sexy look and a bit of flirtation, the next step in a wonderful sequence of lovemaking might be a kiss. Kissing has the potential to lead to more—even from a scientific perspective. Psychologist Gordon Gallup at the University of Albany explains that kissing creates a "situation of proximity" where scents (pheromones) are sniffed and sexy voices and breaths are heard. Kissing is not only tactile; when a man kisses you, he deposits a little bit of his saliva, which contains testosterone—necessary for your arousal. Consequently, a lot of kissing means a lot of testosterone for you and a higher likelihood of sexual intimacy.

Sexual Self-Assessment

As in curing stress addiction, the first step for tapping into desire and pleasure is to gain self-awareness. Answer the following questions to see where your love thermometer stands.

1. Do you have sex two to three times a week?

    ___ Yes ___ No

2. If you don't have an orgasm, do you feel that you still enjoyed the intimacy?   ___ Yes ___ No

3. Are you comfortable being naked?   ___ Yes ___ No

4. Do you openly ask for what you want?   ___ Yes ___ No

5. Are you available for sex, meaning that you don't go to bed early or play dead to avoid having sex?   ___ Yes ___ No

6. Do you forget about or let go of what your spouse has done wrong before sex or during sex?   ___ Yes ___ No

7. Do you schedule plenty of time for sex?   ___ Yes ___ No

8. Do you ever masturbate?   ___ Yes ___ No

9. Do you like erotic movies?   ___ Yes ___ No
10. Do you like to talk "dirty"?   ___ Yes ___ No
11. Do you think about sex during the day out of the blue?

                                                           ___ Yes ___ No
12. Are you content with your sex life, meaning that you are
    not jealous about your girlfriends' sex lives?

                                                           ___ Yes ___ No
13. Do you like sensual pleasures like a pedicure or massage?

                                                           ___ Yes ___ No

If you answered no to five of the questions, you can consider yourself low libido. More than half, and you might think of yourself as nonsexual. However, this would be a big mistake, for how you perceive yourself could become your reality. I hope your answers will help you change where you are today.

But how does this sinking desire get started? The following are some triggers for low libido.

Avoiding Pain

Think back to when you were first awakening to love. Do you remember when you were a young girl and had a crush on someone? Do you also remember how love can really hurt?

Our libido surges during adolescence when our first innocent, genuine encounters with passion are so intense that love hurts. As adults we trade intensity for stability and security—we are self-protective.

"Look what happened to Romeo and Juliet!" we point out. "Better to be safe than sorry." "I don't need to put myself out there to get hurt." "Passion is highly overrated."

Surrendering to Social Conventions

At the same time, your mother, grandmother, or pastor reinforced the theme, "Save yourself for marriage," "Nice girls don't do it," "It's sinful," "It's dirty," "You do it to have children."

Then a major conflict arises: social convention versus our own imagination, a kind of sexual schizophrenia. Where is the middle ground, you wonder? Women in particular have amazing imaginations regarding romance, sex, and relationships. However, if you feel a bit ashamed or even afraid of your imagination, you will censor it. This limits your sexual fire and inhibits your libido. Remember that your internal sexual fire, your fantasies, do not follow a moral code, and when you compel them to adhere to the rules, you constrict, even choke off, your passion.

Increasing Sexual Pleasure and Sensuality

Now that you understand how stress addiction can smother your true life, it's time for some ways to increase your libido and reach a new level of passion and joy with your partner.

Use Your Head

The mind is your most erotic organ. This means you can use your brain to improve your preparation for sex. Rehearse sex in your brain, choreograph it, direct it, and see yourself taking an active role—the way athletes do to pump themselves up before a competition.

Our body responds to imagined realities the way it does to realities. Read sexy, look at sexy, and listen to sexy—in other words, take a targeted multisensory approach to stimulate your imagination. Give your mind permission to travel. Don't judge your imagination as wild and crazy, because this is your liberated libido free from guilt and shame. You certainly don't have to share your fantasies unless you wish. They are your own stories about your innermost desires, dreams, and symbols of your personality—your own myths to dream of.

Don't worry if you are imagining forbidden liaisons. Most likely you won't actually act on them. However, if you con-

TALES OF STRESS ADDICTION

Mirror, Mirror on the Wall

Chris has had two breast augmentations, liposuction, and a face lift; she's had her eyes and neck done and her chin reshaped. She looks great, except that sometimes she has this hollow, vacant look. One day I caught Chris staring at herself in the mirror for a few moments. At first I thought she was being narcissistic. When she noticed me she said, "You know, I still can't recognize myself after all these procedures. I feel like I am looking at a stranger."

Sometimes cosmetic surgery is the unkindest cut of all in the quest to be drop-dead gorgeous. Surgery is always risky business concerning infection, nerve damage, and clots, to name a few. However, cosmetic surgery is also emotionally risky. If you want to look truly beautiful, smile and radiate positive energy.

sciously suppress your fantasies, they will control you in negative ways you never dreamed of. Acknowledge them and decode what they are telling you about yourself: the stimulation you like, the setting, the touch, the position, and the props. Play with them and have an adventure without leaving home.

- Explore your fantasy beforehand to familiarize yourself with it so that you won't be afraid of it or feel that it is strange or awkward. You can always write it down in third person to objectify it and give shape to it—your own romance novel.

- Get your lover involved in the fantasy—as much as you like or are able. You can script the fantasy according to what you feel comfortable doing.

- Read erotic literature. You will conjure up images and see that many of your "strange" fantasies are universal, shared by other women.

- Watch movies that arouse you. If you like porn, well and good, but if you are like many women who don't like hard-core porn, watching romantic and gently erotic movies with a loving message or interesting theme about human nature will help you stimulate your sensuality in a medium that suits your temperament.

- Talk about sex with your girlfriends. Talking gets you going, and you can learn a few things from other women. Remember, your girlfriends can be your therapists.

Tips for Curing Stress Addiction
Avoiding Fantasy Island

It's tempting to escape your real, everyday picture, especially without high-risk consequences. After all, every woman fantasizes about thrilling liaisons with mysterious strangers and celebrities, although not everyone readily admits it. Fantasy becomes a problem, however, when you find yourself escaping into your delicious story more and more as you continue to tune out your spouse. This is known as avoidant coping. When you find yourself turning inward at the expense of your potentially loving reality, then it's time to rein in your escapism and tune in to your reality with your spouse.

Change It Up

Monogamy does not have to mean monotony. You need to bring novelty into your romance. Your slogan for your bedroom should be Expect the Unexpected. Remember that in Step 5 you changed where you sat at the kitchen table to get a different perspective. Similarly, you need to change things up in the bedroom. You can start the process with the simple and concrete:

- In the bedroom, display a photo of the two of you—happy, hugging, and laughing. Get rid of photos of the children or your parents on your night table; they do not belong in your bedroom. If all you have around the lovemaking room are family (group) photos, this speaks volumes about your romantic life.

- How about your bedroom linens—are they worn out or too clinical? You don't have to spend a lot of money to get pretty linens.

- Is your bedroom lighting too harsh? Change the light bulbs to create a softer glow—flattering to the room and to the two of you.

- Is there are a lock on your bedroom door, or can the kids come and go as they please and interrupt you? This is an easy fix.

Next, change what you always wear to bed. Historically, masquerade balls were sensuous events; masks and costumes created an atmosphere of mystery and surprise. Wearing a disguise, you can flirt and say things you normally don't. Although you don't need to wear a Halloween costume in the bedroom (you certainly can if you want to play the French maid), get the props you need to create illusion.

To get yourself emotionally ready for change, cultivate your own rituals that relax you and signal self-nurturing. This will help you to release inhibitions. For example, take a hot bath with lavender, citrus, or vanilla aromatic salts (the three most popular de-stressing fragrances), enjoy a self-massage, and put on a soft, plush robe. Relax into the role you wish to play. If he always initiates, give him an unexpected surprise by initiating this time. If you are always in a hurry, slow down. If you never do a quickie, do a quickie. If you are always on the bed, try the floor, the kitchen counter, the closet, the shower, or the garden.

Because your imagination is so rich, you have a lifetime of fantasies to stage and direct. Have fun!

Push and Pull

If you feel bored in your relationship, you can challenge your emotional balance. Imagine that your spouse might leave you if you are not trying your best to make the relationship work. Visualize some imaginary slithering, manipulative competition and then restabilize and affair-proof your marriage. When you perceive your spouse through the adulterous eyes of another woman,

 Tips for Curing Stress Addiction
The Art of Self-Massage

You feel achy and tired from your long day. For a great pick-me-up and self-nurturing act, give yourself a massage. Warm up some olive oil in the microwave (not too hot) and massage your body. Use long strokes for long limbs and circular movements for the rounded parts of your body. Dab some warm olive oil on your fingers and do what looks like windshield wipers over and under your eyes—your index fingers are lightly positioned at your temples while your thumbs gently glide in a semicircle under your eyes and on top on your eyebrows.

you activate your natural inclination for competition and try harder. You will get great results.

In contrast, if you feel that your spouse is too needy, behaving like a codependent, trying to please a goddess like you, then to spice things up, make him feel more secure. Make him feel loved by being physically and verbally demonstrative. It's show and tell time. Then he will relax, ease up on himself, feel less anxious and more empowered. A man who feels empowered is more exciting in the bedroom.

TALES OF STRESS ADDICTION

The Super Bowl

In the past, Lila always felt neglected and lonely during football season. Ray would watch the climactic Super Bowl stuffing his face with chips, dips, and hero sandwiches, guzzling beer and making a mess. Lila even stood naked, wearing high heels, in front of the TV (as advised in a popular woman's magazine), but Ray only told her to stop blocking his view. She was hurt and angry.

This year's game had a different conclusion. Lila, who knows nothing about football, sat down next to Ray and began to watch TV. He was quite suspicious of her, waiting for the other shoe to drop, when Lila would start to annoy him and ruin this male ritual. "Ray, I want to bet on the game. Tell me the names of the two teams." "You?" "Yes, I want to choose a team, and if my team wins, you fulfill my sexual fantasy when the game is over. If your team wins, I gratify your sexual fantasy." Ray liked the bet, and Lila sat next to Ray excitedly enjoying the game, asking questions and curious about the outcome.

If he is narcissistic and demanding, then demand right back at him. Don't be readily available for him. Upset his balance and act more aloof. Get dressed up and go out with the girls. He will wonder what on earth is going on and work harder to win you over. You will be more exciting to him.

All relationships have a pattern of push and pull. One partner is the pusher and the other is the puller. Reverse the roles that you play.

Communicate Clearly

If you want foreplay outside the bedroom to happen, you need to clearly communicate—no metaphors or hints—what kind and considerate actions you specifically desire. Men are literal creatures and do not use both sides of their brain to process nuances the way you do.

For example, if you want him to clear the table after meals, pick up the heavy laundry basket on the stairs and carry it up, send you an occasional card with a personal message, or make a daily phone call to you from work, then let him know without hinting, pouting, or saying everything is perfectly fine. Schedule his days and duties on a bulletin board in the kitchen.

If he buys you a gift, suppress the conditioned urge to say, "Oh, you shouldn't have," and just thank him warmly and sincerely. If you don't, he might become totally confused and hurt by your lack of appreciation. He needs your approval and physical intimacy to bond with you.

Please note: once you become proficient in the art of expressing what is bothering you, you run the risk of getting caught in a negative loop of anger if you start arguing without a hint of compromise. Repetitive, purposeless arguing is a big turnoff and actually fuels stress, according to marriage guru John Gottman. That's why marriage counseling often fails: the couple spends too much time and emotional energy focusing on processing the neg-

Tips for Curing Stress Addiction
Have a Good Fight

A good fight with your spouse may be good for your health, according to a University of Michigan study. Suppressing anger during a fight, as opposed to expressing anger and resolving the conflict, hastens death. Professor Ernest Harburg, the lead author of the study, explains that couples need to fight and reconcile. Brooding about a hurt or burying your anger causes physiological trouble down the road.

ative. Make sure your conflicts are constructive and then move on. You will learn the art of the good fight in Step 7.

Dress for Success

If you really don't like your body because you are overweight and flabby, do something about it. Step 4 has provided you with the tools for healthy narcissism: balanced eating and exercise. However, if you don't like yourself inside, you will never like your body. Feeling unattractive is a pretty reliable sign that you need to keep working on self-empowerment and on cultivating your unique, distinct identity—growing as an individual.

In the interim, ladies, lingerie goes a long way to hide imperfection. And once you are involved in making love, no one is measuring your body fat ratio with calipers. Dress for success! Dab on the perfume—remember, the smell of grapefruit makes you look younger to him. Give him that sexy look and a radiant smile. Move gracefully, tease him with your touch, and wow—you are so gorgeous! Sensuality is not about beautiful features and a thin body. Sensuality is about the body transmitting your joyous vitality.

Note: you might be in the habit of dressing in baggy, unflattering pants with loose, formula-stained T-shirts during the day. You might be having breakfast with him all disheveled, looking like Brunhilde. Would you dress like this for Brad Pitt or George Clooney? Don't take your spouse and, more important, yourself for granted. What you do during the day affects your nights. And if he is turning you off, sitting unshaven in his underwear—let him know that you would find him more attractive otherwise. Watch him hit the shower, shave, and dress for you—real fast.

Stay Sexually High

The sexual high replaces the high of stress addiction—and it is healthy for you.

Stress addiction diminishes your life force. According to Taoist philosophy, the only energy force that can increase your overall vitality and creativity is sexual energy.

When you recharge your energy with your personal joy, you will be able to be more giving in the bedroom. Have a romance with life by slowing down; take the time to see, feel, and absorb the beauty all around you and, most important, to nurture yourself. When you are not depleted, you will access the most potent source of your happiness, vitality, and health—your uninhibited sexuality.

When you go for a physical, your doctor probably asks about your sex life (and if she doesn't, then she should), not because she is nosy, but because how often you have sex is a good gauge of your overall health. Physicians like Mehmet Oz recommend having sex three times a week—at least. Sexual intimacy

- Lowers blood pressure

- Improves the cardiovascular system

- Boosts the immune system

- Provides a nutritional supplement of zinc, calcium, potassium, fructose, and proteins (from semen, the composition of which also acts as an antidepressant)

- Helps speed up wound healing

- Triggers the development of new neurons in the olfactory system from stem cells in the brain

- Alleviates pain from headache, arthritis, and PMS

- Firms the tummy and buttocks

- Reduces weight

- Increases endorphins

- Makes your skin glow

- Helps you fall asleep

- Increases longevity

Work Out

In Step 4 you learned that exercise challenges your mental, emotional, and, of course, physical balance by inducing a stress response that your body is able to manage. Your body gets all fired up under your control, then recovers and returns to homeostasis, reaping great health benefits, such as literally running yourself out of a frenzy and building a higher stress threshold. You might say that our slogan was Turn Stress into Strength. You also learned that acute stress as opposed to chronic stress can be good for you because it wakes up both the body and the mind and triggers a relaxation response. Therefore, when you exercise regularly, you are learning to feel your body and express yourself through your body.

Exercise and sex have a lot in common: sweat, circulation, calorie burn, stress release, and feel-good chemistry.

You have probably realized from your own experience (which, by the way, is supported by research) that you may prefer to talk about sex rather than do it. This poses a relationship problem that exercise can remedy. Exercise will help you learn the anatomical language of love and habituate you to continuous physical expression; in other words, there will be less talk and more action. When you are working out and breathless, there is no talking. In addition, strength training of the large muscle groups in the legs, back, and chest releases testosterone, which increases libido, not just for men but for women too. Added benefits: you will look better, turn back the clock, and cultivate a better self-image. Exercise is your best treatment for low libido—and even prevents it!

Sometimes your heart might be there, but you simply don't feel anything in the "southern hemisphere." You might need a little physical help with arousal to get blood flowing to the genitalia, and I am happy to say that there are wonderful exercises that work well to bring blood to the area. When you perform these exercises regularly, you will also improve your cardiovascular system.

■ ■ ■

1. **Pelvic lifts.** Lie down with your back on the floor and your feet planted firmly on the floor, hip distance apart. With both your shoulders and feet on the floor and your abdominals tight, lift up only your pelvic region like a bridge. Squeeze your glutes tightly as you lift up. Hold for a few seconds and slowly lower to the floor, returning to your starting position where your back touches the floor. Repeat for a set of five. Exhale on exertion. As this gets easier, aim for three sets of five repetitions.

2. **The clam.** To strengthen your inner and outer thighs, lie down on your side tilting your pelvis and knees forward, one

TALES OF STRESS ADDICTION

See Your Spouse with Adulterous Eyes

Amy has been numb from the waist down since age forty-five. She refuses to have sex with her husband, Bill, but will help him masturbate. Amy and Bill are adept at slinging barbs at each other—ever since they were married twenty years ago. However, neither of them would ever consider divorce—there is too much money involved and of course their two teenage children to consider. Amy dresses beautifully and has a gorgeous face, but she is obese. Bill, who is in decent shape, feels that she should diet more rigorously if she cares about him.

In the past, Amy didn't care much if her husband had a tryst or two ("As long as he left me alone"), but the last one turned out to be his assistant. She was a single woman only a couple of years younger than Bill, not particularly good looking, but eager to please when the lights were off.

"You know, I didn't think I cared or had any sexual feelings left in me. But knowing that *she* could take my husband away from me set off some spark." I suggested that Amy begin a strength training program at her gym and see a nutritionist.

It is never too late to be fit and healthy. Why wait for another woman confident in her sensuality to have an affair with your husband to get you motivated?

leg on top of the other. Open your legs to form a diamond, then bring your knees together, almost touching, slowly and methodically. Then pull them apart as you visualize moving against a resistance. Lift up and repeat, open and close, slowly and with control. Do not use momentum. Switch sides. Aim for three sets of ten repetitions on each side. Inhale and exhale through the move.

3. **Abdominals.** Lie down on the floor with your knees bent and arms at your sides. Contract your abdominals by pulling your navel in toward your spine. Press your back down into the floor and then lift your shoulders off the floor. Contract, compress, and lift. As you lift from the abdominals, slide your hands up your thighs to your knees as if you were painting your thighs with your hands. Your eyes look up, and you should be able to put an imaginary orange under your chin. Exhale on exertion. This is not a sit-up test or a race. Do these slowly and with control. Focus and make each one count. Aim for three sets of ten to fifteen repetitions.

Work Out Together

It's a great idea to have the object of your desire with you when you're getting physical. Remember: strength-training exercises elevate your testosterone level too. While you are both sweating and with two libidos elevated . . . need I say more?

■ ■ ■

1. **Partner-guided squats.** Squats take on a more sensual meaning as your partner guides you up and down in squat position with your glutes lowering into an imaginary bucket. Push off your heels and keep your back straight, as you do not want to hunch forward. Hold in your abdominals tightly. Because your partner holds your hand, you can go

lower than a traditional squat, and target your glutes more. Your partner determines intensity and tempo by the pressure of his touch. Aim for three sets of ten. If you widen your stance with your toes pointing out, you will target your inner thighs. Now do the same for him and guide his squats. Exhale on exertion.

2. **Tandem lunges.** For a romantic variation of the traditional lunge, hold your partner's left hand with your right, and together do five stationary lunges, coming forward on opposite knees so that you don't bump into each other—unless you want to. When you lunge, the knee going forward is at a ninety-degree angle; your front foot is flat on the floor, and your knee does not extend over the toe. The other leg is behind you, with the knee bent toward the floor but not touching it. Bring your front leg back to your start position—stand straight on both legs. Then switch sides. Remember to exhale on exertion and hold in your abdominals tightly. Begin by doing five to eight repetitions on each side. Aim for three sets.

3. **The ultimate oblique workout.** Stand back-to-back as you pass a basketball or weighted medicine ball (weight to be determined by you) to each other by turning in a smooth twist from side to side. You are synchronizing your body movements to work in harmony. Pass and receive the ball with one hand on top of the ball and the other hand under it. Together you pass the ball full circle. Aim for twenty-five repetitions. As this gets easier, use a heavier ball. Remember to exhale on exertion and hold in your abdominals tightly.

■ ■ ■

If you go to the gym, you can spot one another with free weights and stretch together. Let your body speak for you.

Belly Dance

Earthy movements will help you get in touch with your sensuality. Belly dancing shakes down inhibitions to release core feminine energy. It is not only a great workout for abdominals, back, hips, and legs but also a wonderful emotional release. Whereas ballet movements are angular and elongated, belly dancing is circular and spontaneous, delighting in the roundness of the female form—a full figure is definitely an asset.

Originating in the Middle East, where women went from father's house to husband's house, belly dancing enabled a woman to control her space and express her full range of emotions. Mostly women danced for other women to teach them about life, love, sex, birth, and feminine creativity. Dance for yourself and then for your beloved. You can learn a few moves from a video. Just tie a scarf around your hips, wear a necklace, and let yourself go.

Your belly dancing sensuality, as in dancing to Afro-Caribbean rhythms, is in your pelvic region; it is expressed in earthy movements performed lower to the ground, with bent knees. I have seen women of all shapes and sizes in my belly dancing classes; at first they are shy and inhibited, then they really cut loose and let their hair down. Warning: when you dance for your husband, you might not get to finish the dance.

Enjoy the Love Diet

Throughout the ages, certain foods have been reputed to be aphrodisiacs. Oysters are one of the most popular. Nutritionists say that they are rich in zinc, which increases libido. Asparagus, aside from its being a phallic symbol and a finger food, is rich in folate necessary for histamine production, which helps you have orgasms. Garlic contains allicin, which increases blood flow to sexual organs. Herbs and spices, such as Korean ginseng, which improves blood flow to the genitals and stimulates energy, are said to make you sensual. Chili pepper and ginger improve circulation. Hot spices like cumin, curry, and cayenne raise your heart rate and make you sweat—similar to the physical reaction to sex. For occasional coffee drinkers, coffee boosts libido, but if you drink a lot daily, you won't reap the same benefit.

Having said all this, however, I have to point out that according to the FDA, all claims about the aphrodisiac properties of foods are based on folklore, not fact. John Renner, founder of the Consumer Health Information Research Institute, calls the mind a potent aphrodisiac. Oysters come from the sea, so think Aphrodite, goddess of love. Ginseng root also has a phallic appearance. Bear in mind too that the placebo effect can be quite potent. Even eating a banana can be a sensual experience, depending how you peel it and bite into it. But that doesn't necessarily make a banana an aphrodisiac. Fact or folklore, you decide.

Scientists advise you to adhere to the so-called Mediterranean diet. Several studies have found an association between obesity with pronounced abdominal fat and the development of metabolic syndrome, whose constellation of abnormalities includes diabetes and cardiovascular disease. Strong evidence links the

---

 Tips for Curing Stress Addiction
Chocolate: A Seductive Treat

Chocolates used to be a treat for the noble classes and were considered aphrodisiacs because they tasted so good and were rare. Italian researchers claim that dark chocolate is an aphrodisiac because it possesses a "love chemical," phenylethylamine, which boosts energy and mood. In their surveys, women who ate more chocolate were more sexual. Chocolate also improves circulation. I love dark chocolate, so all this works for me!

risk of erectile dysfunction in men and sexual problems in women with metabolic syndrome. This makes sense if insufficient blood is flowing to the pelvic region. After switching to a Mediterranean diet—a variety of fruits, vegetables, whole grains, legumes, nuts (especially walnuts), and olive oil; a glass of red wine daily; and very little red meat, refined grains, and processed foods—both men and women score far higher on standardized indices of sexual function.

Reject Those Myths

Aren't you tired of "conventional wisdom," those old wives' tales that drag us down into sexual inertia and passion paralysis? Here are a few of them, along with the cure:

1. *Sex has to be spontaneous.* Sometimes sex is spontaneous, but mostly it isn't, especially when there are work, children, and extended family to take into consideration. Plan ahead for sex and enjoy the anticipation.

2. *My partner should fulfill me entirely, and since he doesn't, I need to find my true soul mate.* People often turn to other partners hoping to find their own significance. This rarely works. Your partner cannot satisfy every single one of your needs or provide you with a new personality or psychological makeover. When you don't grow as a person or maintain your distinct separateness, you lose your opportunity for happiness. You do not find your significance in a significant other. But when you find your empowerment within, you bring this new sense of self to your relationship. As a person who is continuing to grow, you are excitingly sensual to your partner.

3. *Out of sight, out of mind.* In many cases, the opposite is true. Abstinence does make the heart grow fonder! You don't have to abstain for a long period of time (unlike a couple living in a non-divorce, who have put off sex for so long that

TALES OF STRESS ADDICTION

No More Nagging

Stacy and Joe had stopped having sex. Because she was in menopause, she felt that she no longer needed it, and Joe was no stallion, exciting and hot to trot. Stacy's perception was actually a classic case of projection: Joe still found Stacy desirable, but because he hated being rejected all the time, he stopped pursuing her.

Interesting. Stacy's chief complaint about their relationship was that Joe never fixed things around the house like he used to. He loved to putter and do projects around the house, but he became unresponsive to her nagging about all the handyman jobs. Then one evening after dinner and a glass of wine in a beautiful restaurant, Joe kissed Stacy passionately when they arrived home. To his happy surprise, she responded, and both of them enjoyed making love. The next day, without Stacy's saying a word, Joe was doing home improvement projects again. He just wanted to please her and couldn't do enough for her. She never had to nag again. A lack of response in one department can lead to a lack of response in another—tit for tat, even on a subconscious level.

they are completely off track). A few days off creates anticipation and eagerness. You might love steak, but having it
every night diminishes the gustatory pleasure. Declare a brief
period of celibacy, and you will both be driven crazy with
desire for forbidden fruit.

Habituate yourself to regular sex, but don't ever let love become a routine, a robotic obligatory habit. You didn't just fall in
love with your significant other because he was immensely attractive. He became attractive to you because you fell in love with
him and enjoyed the whole idea of love.

TALES OF STRESS ADDICTION
Using Viagra

Sonia and Carl, in their early fifties, are both healthy and lead
an active lifestyle. In fact, they don't look their age. Lately Carl
was having trouble maintaining an erection during their lovemaking. He was beginning to feel anxious about having sex, so
he started going to bed later, after Sonia was asleep. Sonia felt
undesirable. After a couple of months, Sonia and Carl were taking an after-dinner walk in the park when Sonia finally had the
courage to bring up the sensitive issue.

"Carl, I was wondering if there is anything I could do so
that we could be intimate again. I miss you." Carl looked into
Sonia's teary eyes. "Is this what you have been thinking, that
it's you? No, I'm having a problem. It's my problem. I think I'm
getting old."

■ ■ ■

Love is truly a mind and body experience. Keep in mind that during all phases of lovemaking when we are vulnerably exposed, we are hypersensitive and suggestible. This is why it is important to be kind to each other. In Step 7, the highest rung of the ladder, I will demonstrate the art of constructive conflict, which leads to compassion and forgiveness—the ultimate lightness of being.

"No way, honey! You're in great shape and a good athlete. Why don't you go to the doctor, get yourself checked out, and maybe to get things going again ask for some Viagra. Janet's husband uses it. Besides, I'll make it worth your while."

Carl was a little hesitant, but Sonia was endearing; he made the appointment. Sonia and Carl are now just like two honeymooners—relaxed, slow, and stress-free.

As of 2001, fourteen million prescriptions of Viagra have been dispensed, and the male population receiving those prescriptions is getting younger. Note that men at any age experience erectile dysfunction from time to time. If it becomes a persistent issue, the underlying causes might be a hormonal imbalance, cardiovascular problems, diabetes, prostate problems, or stress.

A visit to the doctor can change your life. When you work this problem out as a team, the treatment is highly successful. My male friends tell me that Viagra eliminates performance anxiety and improves long-lasting lovemaking.

Reframe Your Thoughts

Now we are ready for Step 7, silencing the bullies in our head and stifling that stern inner critic. I want each and every one of you reading this book to become skilled at reframing the thoughts that upset you, erode who you are as an individual, and sap your positive inner energy. I don't want you to drag around a leg iron of worry and anger wherever you go. Imagine how free and joyous you can feel when you activate your potential for optimism, enabling you to bounce resiliently back from conflicts, setbacks, and crises.

The Power of Thought

Have you ever noticed that when a past hurt flits across your consciousness, your heart races, a flush suffuses your neck, and your breathing speeds up from the mere thought? When I was a teenager, I recall my mother relating an argument she had had with her sister Hannah. I was shocked to see my mother, usually composed and cheerful, breathless and with the artery in her neck pulsating. "When did Aunt Hannah do this to you?"

"Oh, it was about eighteen years ago."

"Eighteen years ago? But Ma . . . Why are you so upset now?"

"Every time I remember it, I still feel enraged. I can't believe I let her get away with it. Keep in mind that a leopard doesn't change its spots."

The Importance of Changing Old Stories

You possess the ability to let old hurts go. You can even detoxify an old painful memory, ancient history, to finally get rid of the hurt by simply changing the story. You can revise your life story, making it better and better as you go along, gathering more objective information by questioning family and friends, learning to have fun with it, and discovering all kinds of amazing thoughts you never realized you had. Compare the powerful impact of your negative thoughts to the upsetting emotions a nightmare evokes. The process of letting go is similar to what you might do if your child were having a nightmare. He wakes up terrified over some wild fantasy. You respond to his cries of distress, reassuring him by challenging the nightmarish thought. You alter the scary elements and befriend the monster to reshape the ending into a happy one. Your child feels better and goes back to sleep, having let the nightmare go.

We all hear voices—good ones and bad ones—in our heads. Isn't it logical to filter out the bad voices? We know that if we have a pain in the body, the more we focus on the pain, the more it hurts and makes us irritable and negative. When we are distracted or give our attention to the things we enjoy, the pain can miraculously dissipate. The same principle applies to emotional pain.

Make a commitment to cultivating internal peace. Don't wait for external circumstances to create peace for you, because peace and serenity begin in your mind and emanate outward. If it's a rainy day, let your inner light shine out. You can quiet your mind and induce happiness any time you wish. Just use your head.

No One Upsets You But You

We tend to see in others traits similar to our own. And when we get angry, often it is something within ourselves we don't like. To relax and feel happier, we need to face this important truth about anger: no one upsets you but you. When you hold on to anger and can't forgive, you diminish your capacity for joy. You hurt yourself. It's often ourselves whom we can't forgive.

Most things that upset your equilibrium challenge your self-image. However, when you know who you are and what you bring to the table, you tend not to get upset, or if you do, at least you can regain your composure quickly. It's time to take responsibility for feeling upset. For example, the other day a car cut me off on the highway and then slowed down right in front of me. Hey—if you're going to cut me off, at least speed up and keep pace. My first reaction was, "The nerve of that guy to cut me off like that. I need to show him who's boss."

Fortunately, I quickly switched mental gears. "Why am I annoyed? No one is doing anything to me. The driver doesn't even know me." I drove on, and a couple of miles down the road, I passed the car to exit the highway. I couldn't resist the urge to stare condescendingly at the driver. Apparently I hadn't completely let it go. The driver happened to be an elderly woman—a hollow victory.

The equivalent of road rage can also occur at home with your spouse and children. For example, your boss criticized your work at the office, the commute home was delayed, and you're late with dinner. Suddenly, you spy your daughter's jacket in the mid-

Tips for Curing Stress Addiction
Road Rage

There's more road rage than ever before. Peter Kissinger, president of the American Automobile Association's Foundation for Traffic Safety, reports that hundreds of motorists are being shot, stabbed, or run over for totally stupid reasons, such as "She wouldn't let me pass" or "Nobody gives *me* the finger." And many of the people committing road rage out there are successful people with no prior history, like a doctor from the Mayo Clinic who was found guilty of vehicular homicide. Kissinger explains that the accumulation of stress for hard-working people compels them to emotional and physical violence that is totally out of character for them. "Something seems to just snap when a motorist doesn't move as soon as the light turns green."

dle of the living room, and you vent all your frustration on her; it's quite a tirade, leaving her in tears. As a result, you are angry at yourself for losing it. If you had regained your balance, you wouldn't have overreacted to the jacket; you would have asked your daughter to hang it up and help you with dinner.

There are basically two people we need to forgive in order to let go and live. The obvious one is the perpetrator. The more significant one is the self. Once we forgive ourselves for our own failures, we will be emotionally available to forgive others. However, the hardest person to feel compassion for is the self. Even when you feel depressed, you don't feel compassion for yourself. On the contrary, you feel guilty for feeling sad, berating yourself for bringing everyone else down around you. To avoid depression, the sword that is aimed inward, you need to speak up, turn the sword outward, then return it to its scabbard.

 Tips for Curing Stress Addiction

Irreconcilable Differences

From an evolutionary standpoint, human survival has always depended on our ability to stay together and cooperate, whether while hunting, cultivating crops, protecting each other from physical danger, or supporting one another emotionally and creating social contracts. We thus have a strong impulse toward compassion and forgiveness as a means of avoiding potentially violent conflict. Because it is human nature to transgress against the people closest to us, reconciliation must follow. According to Martin Seligman, the leader of the positive psychology movement, unresolved conflict, particularly in families, can become downright unhealthy, causing depression and anxiety. Your happiness depends on your ability to get along with people. When you are compassionate, you are actually being selfish (in a good way!). Is there someone, such as a family member, friend, or coworker, with whom you can repair a bridge?

Anger Management

The goal in anger management is not to pretend that everything is just fine, or to brush the anger off our shoulders and act as if nothing bothers us. If we are honest about it, most of us feel things more intensely than we would care to admit to others, for to reveal the truth might be perceived as a sign of weakness. "Nah, it doesn't bother me that you've found a convenient excuse to avoid carpool duty this whole month. I can continue to do it with the new baby and all." You might be surprised to learn that human doormats have a great deal of suppressed anger. Resentment surfaces at odd times to overwhelm us and causes physical inflammation that disrupts our immune system. Because it acts on the entire central nervous system like an amphetamine, anger is always followed by a physiological crash.

Don't shrink from expressing your emotions, but do work to get over them quickly. You can use anger to drive full speed ahead or to keep spinning your wheels. Laboratory experiments have shown that even subtle forms of anger weaken problem-solving abilities and overall competence. In addition to increasing errors, anger narrows and paralyzes your mental focus, tending to eclipse options. This might leave you feeling helpless and hopeless. You can choose to get past this sticking point by removing the stinger.

Changing the Story

It's human nature to create stories about everything. In situations where we don't really know all the details or remember what actually happened, we tend to make up details that we then take as facts, blurring the lines between fact and fiction. However, note that your subjective stories change according to your changing life situation. The more self-confident you are, the kinder the interpretation. And kindness, generosity of spirit to others, for-

TALES OF STRESS ADDICTION
Moving Day

Nancy got divorced, and moved to a new apartment. She was also battling breast cancer and felt fatigued from the radiation. Nancy was furious with her best friend, Emily, who did not help her move. "What kind of friend is that?" Every week during our cancer stress management workshop, she vented about the perceived betrayal.

A month later, Nancy sheepishly related that Emily threw her an elaborate surprise party. Nancy was touched by all the effort and finally let go of her resentment. Her angry interpretation almost cost her a friendship that had begun in high school. "Still, I would have preferred that Emily help me move rather than throw me a surprise party." Nancy should have spoken up and asked her friend to help her move. Friends are not clones or mind readers.

tifies your self-worth, enabling you to create more positive stories. Stories with good plots and happy endings facilitate forgiveness, a lightness of being. Creating a positive story is a two-pronged approach to coping with anger directed toward perceived injustices. First, you are able to forgive both yourself and the transgressor, which releases your internally driven stress, allowing you to move on. Second, the more you practice the "art" of forgiving, putting a compassionate spin on the upset, the more automatic the process becomes, which prevents a great deal of anger. It's always easier to prevent than to treat.

- To facilitate the process of forgiveness, examine
  what you are telling yourself. Do you lean to the
  negative or the positive? Can you open up to
  another person's point of view and accept a differing
  opinion?

- Do you expect more from other people than you do
  from yourself? What is really bothering you—that
  someone hurt you or that you allowed yourself to
  be hurt?

Doing It Better Like a Buddhist

Buddhists practice living in the moment using their five senses. While a Buddhist is contemplating the spirit world, he is very much aware of the crack in the sidewalk and will not trip, because he is completely present and not stuck in a bad thought or worry that can undermine his alertness. Remember how heavy it felt to hold even briefly that half-full glass? Put it down. Buddhists cultivate positivism by transforming negative situations, hostile words, or images into positives. The premise is that no one knows the absolute truth. We all see things from our own perspectives, and many interpretations could be right at the same time. Buddhists regularly practice conjuring up a terrible imagined scenario, then reinterpreting it with a positive spin. Because they practice reinterpretation frequently, it becomes a natural mind-set, an instinct. Why can't you choose the optimistic interpretation? The more you practice, the more you will rewire your brain until it becomes an automatic response.

Putting a Positive Spin on Real Life

Let's examine a few disturbing thoughts that you might have.

- Life is unfair. Why do I have to struggle financially?
  My kids are deprived.

TALES OF STRESS ADDICTION

Practice What You Preach

I was running a workshop on anger management with a French trainer, Monique, who was chosen to lead the closing meditation because of her beautiful, lyrical voice. We had a large group set up in a gym studio that was, unfortunately, only a couple of rooms away from a racquetball court. Monique had begun the meditation, and the participants were soon relaxed, breathing deeply. Suddenly, wham, bang, slam against the wall. She winced, but continued in her singsong voice. Next, the door was opened by someone from the reception desk: "Will the owner of a silver Toyota Camry please move your car, as you are blocking the exit?"

Monique exploded, "Mais non, I can't do this! Who can possibly meditate here under these ridiculous circumstances?" To confess, I was a bit embarrassed by the irony of my copresenter's outburst during a stress management session, and it was the last time we worked together. However, I had to salvage the situation on the spot, so I jumped in and proclaimed in my brightest sunshine voice, "This is a great example of the real conditions of meditation, because we don't meditate in a cocoon. When you meditate at home, the phone rings or your child tugs at your sleeve. You can always begin again by noting your surroundings, closing your eyes, and breathing to your own natural rhythm. Let's try this again."

- My son was rejected from the college of his choice. I feel terrible for him.

- I was so embarrassed when my husband said in front of our friends, "You don't know what you're talking about!" Now they think I'm stupid.

Let's reinterpret these thoughts with a compassionate spin.

- I would prefer life to be fair, but is life really fair? It's true that I work hard and need more money. I can update my skills to climb the ranks or find a higher-paying job elsewhere. Who says that my kids are deprived if they don't have the latest designer clothes or gadgets? Maybe they are rich in values.

- I want the best for my child, but cannot take away his disappointments. Actually, rejection can build character. Everyone gets rejected in life. He will go to college, just not this one, and he will be motivated to do his best and to prove himself. He can get a good education in any accredited school.

- My husband must have been stressed about something at work, and my words accidentally hit a raw nerve. While it is true that he should be more polite and evaluate his words in front of our friends, he really didn't mean to make me look bad. My friends know my capabilities. Later I will make him aware that I felt hurt and that he should consider his words more carefully. Also, I will ask him what is really bothering him and if I can help.

Be prepared that sometimes the people you interact with are going to be just plain ornery or at best difficult; accept that there

TALES OF STRESS ADDICTION

Put Out the Fire

Vickie was not in the Christmas spirit. "My husband, Greg, brought home my Christmas present, and at first I thought it was a disaster. My best friend, Carla, had received a diamond pendant, and I took the time to find Greg a special cashmere sweater and the hottest new cologne. We exchanged our gifts eagerly, but when I unwrapped mine, I was surprised. Stunned, in fact, since it wasn't a beautiful piece of jewelry or lovely thing to wear, but a bright red fire extinguisher! A fire extinguisher! I was fuming!"

Perhaps Vickie should spray that fire extinguisher on her self to put out the inflammation! How could she reinterpret this angry moment? Maybe like this: "How thoughtful of my husband to buy me a fire extinguisher because he loves me so dearly! Greg knows I don't feel safe when he goes off on a business trip." Vickie laughed and agreed with me when she heard this, realizing that Greg is a sweet guy who loves gadgets and probably sees himself as a knight in shining armor.

is nothing you can do to change them except through your behavior. Getting rid of your anger will help you consider your options, to stay or go. Ranting at someone rarely improves behavior. Often it fuels the other person's anger, and you then have an incendiary situation on your hands. Remember, as in the case of your daughter and her jacket in the middle of the room, the biggest regret you feel afterwards is that you lost your temper. What helps cool down anger is empathy. Forgive your daughter and let her rectify the situation. Understand what someone else is feeling while you maintain your own separate emotions. Bring out the best in others. This neutralizes the tension. When you understand the needs of another, you lose your anger and regain a vital connection.

You can reinterpret the motives of complete strangers and forgive them, which allows them to make amends. Suppose that at a restaurant one evening, your waiter first ignores you, then gets your order wrong and refuses to admit it. You are fuming, thinking thoughts like "The waiter hates me. The waiter has it in for me. I will leave him a dollar as a tip." The only thing these hostile thoughts will give you is indigestion. To reinterpret with compassion, think to yourself, "The waiter has a big station and has worked a long, hard day. He probably has a lot of problems at home." See, it's not about you. You might turn the tables by expressing compassion while you gently communicate your displeasure: "I'm sorry that you are overloaded and having a hard day. Could you please return this order to the chef, as I wanted it well done . . ." "Yes, of course, I'm sorry. I'll get to it immediately. And please accept a free dessert tonight with an after-dinner drink."

Forgiving the Unforgivable

Learning how to put a positive spin on human foibles, those little indiscretions or thoughtless acts that were not meant to harm,

TALES OF STRESS ADDICTION

Mother-in-Law from Hell

Mothers-in-law are one of the most pervasive thorns in family relationships and one of the most potent button pushers we will ever meet. I have heard countless complaints, such as this one: "My mother-in-law refuses to acknowledge me, never calls me by my first name, and at best, addresses me as 'Hey you.' She disagrees with the way I raise the children and criticizes my cooking, the way I dress, and how I talk to my husband, her wonderful son. She is always giving me unsolicited advice. When I don't follow her orders, she claims that I don't like her."

To reinterpret, try to cut her some slack, as this is a case of two women in love with the same man. Your husband loves you and lives with you. Your mother-in-law carried him for nine months and raised him to be the man you love. She deserves a space in his heart. You can be magnanimous and civil without following her advice. Here are some ideas for winning her over: Schedule one-on-one time to get to know her better. You just might discover who she really is. Ask her about her dreams and longings when she was your age or even a young girl.

Do an activity together—one that *she* likes. When you are having fun together, she will loosen up and see you in a different light.

When she slings a few barbs your way, deflect them by changing the subject to something positive, such as the children or her son.

is relatively easy when you are aware and do not get lost in the confusion of anger: in these cases it's no problem for you to forgive others and take the high road. However, reinterpreting more significant hurts with compassion in order to forgive . . . well, that's another matter. As in most aspects of stress management, you begin with the small stressors and habituate to managing them. Then you turn each new, more challenging stressor into a new strength.

Of course, it's much easier to forgive others when they profusely apologize and renounce their transgressions, vowing to make amends. However, even if people don't own up or apologize, you can still let go if you reframe even the worst of transgressions, such as sexual abuse. For example, I asked Edwene Gaines, author and motivational speaker, how she healed from the brutality of sexual abuse that she experienced from infancy until age four. In fact, she almost died because of it. Edwene explained that she held on to the anger, fear, and self-pity long into her adult years, unable to let go, until she found a way to rewrite her terrible story. "In my new story, I went from victim to victor. I was abused as a kind of initiation into power. Because I possess enormous power, having been abused taught me to use this power to help others, and never misuse my power to hurt anyone. I can survive anything and do anything, for I am that strong."

"Isn't this a bit of a reach?" I asked her. "Sounds to me like some crazy story you made up to let the abuser off the hook, without any truthful basis."

"Perhaps, but you see, this is a story I can live with, and in my life I can make up stories as I go along. Perceiving myself as a victor helped me to finally get past it all. Is self-pity a better version?"

Reframing is all about centering yourself for a more optimistic outlook. Once you announce your reality, you have had your say and gotten it off your chest. If you choose to forgive the transgressor, you are able to let things go in order to be at peace.

Remember, healthy narcissists do not hold on; they move away from toxicity.

Calming Down

When you first start implementing the technique of reframing your thoughts, you might feel too angry to reinterpret a conflict or a harsh word. Don't worry; you will get the hang of it. Use what you learned in Step 2 to calm down: take ten deep breaths, inhaling two counts and exhaling four counts through the nose to oxygenate your brain and slow down your pulse so that you can think more clearly. If at all possible, remove yourself for a short while and walk it off. This will help move the anger right out of your body while releasing endorphins to help you feel your way to the sunnier side. At this point you will be able to reinterpret the situation more objectively. Instead of dwelling on who is wrong and what was done to you, you can redirect your thoughts to "How can I let this go? I have better things to think about."

How to Have a Constructive Conflict

Reframing your thoughts with greater compassion and understanding will not eliminate inevitable disagreements and heated debates. Even if you are not upset with others, they might be upset with you. You can be drained by their negative energy. You will need to fortify yourself to become immune to their negative words and quickly divert their personal attacks. Because you have a strong self-concept, you can validate everyone's right to think and talk in his or her own way. Once you tear someone's ego down in an argument, the conflict spirals out of control. Also, it is sometimes necessary to tolerate uncertainty and ambiguity— no definitive answers. From your personal frame of reference, you will notice that as your responsibilities multiply, life accelerates, and your equilibrium becomes harder to maintain; you give others only partial attention, unable to really listen. This is the busy intersection where mistakes and misunderstandings multiply. This is when you must realize that enough is enough. Chronic stress is bullying your positive perceptions. You need to take command of yourself to slow down, evaluate the perceived transgressions, and find a pragmatic solution to reconcile those differing opinions.

Fighting for Change

Clearly, your natural rhythm is not always in sync with others. So instead of tallying up every remark or action, try allowing all the people in your life to be who they are and not forcing them to be just what you want! The goal is to adapt to situations and people, not impose yourself on them—to influence them without controlling or manipulating them. This doesn't mean that you please others by suppressing your honest opinions. Instead, you can show respect for other people's opinions without necessarily agreeing with them.

It's not how often you argue, but how you argue that matters in your relationships with others. The way you handle conflicts, your personal style of arguing, will predict your success. Never lose sight of your goal, which is a constructive solution, a change for the better, and sometimes even accepting a differing opinion because you have learned a thing or two. People who are always right scare me.

When it comes to religion and politics, you know the rules—tiptoe around the other person's views and avoid getting embroiled in a useless verbal brawl where no one's opinion will ever change. All you have to do is listen attentively and respond—not react.

Seizing the Right Moment

During a skirmish, you want to act like a leader and direct the course of the battle for a successful outcome, as opposed to reacting to someone else's strategies. When you argue, in a matter of

seconds you will be pegged as good or bad or as a loser or a winner. That's just how it is, for people make snap judgments based
on looks, body language, and tone and not just the facts, as
Malcolm Gladwell explains in *Blink*. Proper timing can lead to a
surer victory than almost any persuasive argument. Because if your
rhythm is out of sync with the other person's, you are losing the
advantage of common ground, as similarity influences likability.
Make sure to build a rapport with the "enemy" to work things out.
Don't undermine your own efforts to win this conflict by over-
looking a few simple strategies. Here are some basic principles to
consider for fighting fair and avoiding permanent damage.

- Is this a good time for the other person to hear
  what you have to say? Just because you are ready to
  speak doesn't mean he or she has the time to listen.
  Do not pounce because you are all fired up. Wait!
  Breathe deeply, exercise, or speak to a positive
  friend. When you are calmer and have a little
  distance, you will be thinking more clearly.

- What is the other person's mood? Relaxed or
  impatient, insecure, pessimistic, stressed, or hungry?
  Put the focus on the other person. Think of the
  consequences.

- Is your argument going nowhere or degenerating
  into a shouting match? Consider changing location
  by simply taking it into another room; by changing
  the environment, you subliminally cause the other
  person to switch gears.

- Are you drawing on your intimate knowledge of a
  husband or friend to hit below the belt? Using family
  secrets you know someone is ashamed of isn't fair,
  and you know it. Remember the concept of empathy. In order for someone to like you, you have to
  like him or her.

Although many of you have been struggling for years to finally open up and say what's on your mind, remember to think before you speak, because as Emily Dickinson pointed out, "a word said is never dead."

The Art of Listening Without Interrupting

We speak all the time to make ourselves heard, to cry for attention. When we disagree or express a personal opinion, we love to be right. We think that in order to be right, we must make the other person wrong. We might use logic, raise our voice, or become sarcastic. Basically, many of us only pretend to listen as we tune out the other person while we think of what we want to say. We also have a habit of interrupting people during a conversation, especially during a heated conflict. Often you hear, "Could you please let me finish? Then you can talk." Why do we interrupt? Here are some typical reasons:

- I'm going to forget what I have to say, and it's brilliant. You're speaking too slowly.

- I know what you are going to say. I've heard it all before.

- I'm passionate about what I have to say. I just have to jump in here.

- You're having trouble finding the right word. I'll help you.

When you really listen to others, you may well be surprised by what you learn. Quite often people don't have a clear idea of what their point is until they keep talking and finally hit on it. If you interrupt, you stop them from completing the thought. Listening levels the playing field, as it shows the other person that you are willing to learn and improve.

Try spending some time with family and friends just listening. You are allowed to respond to their questions, but you are not allowed to initiate or jump into the conversation. See what happens. Did anyone even notice or miss anything?

Victory Can Defeat You

When you are engaged in a conflict, instead of trying so hard to prove the other person wrong and yourself right, you can try to be open to learning more about the other perspective. When you hear the other side, you can often enlarge your own perspective to see that perhaps the other viewpoint has some merit. Sometimes you win when you lose the argument! In other words, you win when you apologize or if you feel that perhaps you are partially wrong. However, if you still believe that you are right, listening to what the other person is saying can improve your ability to strengthen your position. You can completely disarm a spouse or boss's arsenal of opinion when he hears his own words coming back at him. When you argue, it is important to understand that human nature makes us see ourselves in a better light to protect our own egos. Everyone lies to herself and believes those lies. In our own faulty memories, we have always behaved better and been nobler, braver, cleverer, kinder, or more innocent than everyone else. (Isn't it interesting how you and your sibling could have two different memories of the same event?) That's why you have to step back, pause, and stop yourself from always justifying your actions and insisting that others do everything your way.

For example, if you put yourself on a pedestal, a suffering, virtuous woman, you can be brutal when itemizing every mistake your spouse has ever made. This is the time to pause for a few moments to avoid those biting remarks, because they show your contempt. When he hears your contempt he wonders, "How can someone who has contempt for me possibly love me?"

Take the Last Laugh

Humor can be an excellent tool for transforming a very dark or negative conflict into a silly or absurd moment of ironic insight.

Tips for Curing Stress Addiction
How Do You Fight?

Let's identify your personal fighting style and see what it reveals about you. Do you fit into any of these four basic categories?

1. **The Boxer.** You take the tit-for-tat approach, firing back immediately with an insult. You fight to win and go for the knockout punch! Your use of the Boxer style suggests that you might feel insecure. This is why you swiftly administer justice by teaching your partner a well-deserved lesson. You don't let any remark fall by the wayside, and might resort to name-calling.

2. **The Smiler.** You smile while you hold a dagger behind your back. You pretend that everything is okay and that you are not hurt. However, you hold a grudge as you plot revenge. Then, when no one expects it, you punish your opponent by not participating in something he or she would enjoy. If you are the Smiler, you are a people pleaser and have a hard time expressing your true feelings.

For example, my husband, Steve, and I had driven five hours in the pouring rain from New York to Boston to attend a big family dinner hosted by my sister-in-law. As she set up the serving trays in her immaculate kitchen, my sister-in-law turned to me and said, "Debbie, did you know that I take notes after every dinner party to keep a record of what my guests like to eat? And I have a note in my journal here that you love dark chocolate." I was quite relieved by the innocuous comment. At least she didn't have anything bad on me, and who knows, I might get some chocolate for dessert. Sure enough, after dinner she brought out this beautiful edible chocolate basket filled with assorted tantalizing chocolate goodies and put it in the middle of the table. I reached out to snatch one and unwrap the gold crepe wrapper.

You masquerade because you want to be well liked, but you are angry. During a fight you are ambivalent about speaking your mind, and give off mixed signals.

3. **The Stonewaller.** You are passive-aggressive. Like the Smiler, you say, "Nothing is wrong. I'm fine after all!" However, you say this without a smile; your opponent can clearly see that something is definitely wrong. When he or she tries to test the waters with cheerful conversation, you reply using one- or two-word answers. You distance yourself by hanging out alone, closing the door, and freezing the other person out.

4. **The Diplomat.** You are a great politician and know how to diffuse the situation. You preface any disagreement or criticism with a compliment or two, affirming your opponent and disarming him or her before you get into it. The Diplomat knows how to manipulate others through flattery, some of it false. Sometimes you tend to control others, who get bamboozled into your solution.

"Oh no, Deb, these are not for you. They are a table decoration. I'm saving them for next week's company. Would you like some fruitcake or marble cake?"

I couldn't believe it. "Let me get this straight. You mean to say you're not going to let me have one little piece of chocolate?" The pitch of my voice was rising. I thought seriously about knocking her unconscious with the candlestick or wrestling her to the ground. My husband watched me intently. He knew that no one got between me and my chocolate.

"Oh no," she went on. "I need these hand-dipped chocolates for next week. You will just have to take no for an answer." She smirked, throwing down her napkin on the table like a gauntlet. Well, I felt like storming out of the room; however, the rest of the family was happily eating the other desserts.

"On second thought, I'll have some marble cake." I took some of the soft, spongy cake, rolled it up into a ball, and threw it at her. My aim was pretty good—right between the eyes. "Put that in your notes about this year's dinner!" We both laughed, and the hostilities ended. Even when you feel powerless, humor gives you some power.

Then there was the time when Steve and I and our friends Joey and his wife, Annette, were staying in this idyllic hotel in the Canadian Rockies. Joey had just gotten off the phone with his broker, who had given him some grim news. Also, we were experiencing some unusually hot weather in the Rockies—without any air conditioning. We were having breakfast, and the waitress, a sweet little college student, accidentally splashed a couple of drops of orange juice on Joey's lap. A little water on a napkin would have easily taken care of it. Instead, Joey threw a hissy fit. He called the manager over, berating the service. The three of us felt bad for the waitress. Joey just wouldn't let up. The manager offered to dry-clean his shorts, promising to have them ready later in the day. I had to interrupt. "Joey, take off your pants and give them to this nice manager!"

"What? Here? Now?" Joey looked at me frowning at first, murderous it seemed, then beginning to grin and finally laughing hysterically. He apologized to the manager and the waitress. After breakfast we all hiked to one of the most beautiful glacial ponds we'd ever seen.

Tips for Constructive Conflict

- Limit communicating your position to two minutes and stick to the facts. Otherwise you risk straying from the topic, repeating yourself, or venting. Be flexible while the discussion unfolds; be ready to change your mind or else come up with different evidence to support emerging issues.

- Tap into your opponent's value system. Summarize his point of view to show that you respect him. It will cool him off to hear you reiterate his words— without sarcasm. "If I understand you correctly . . ." Try to predict a future outcome. This can be highly persuasive because you are imagining a possible result (no pressure here), and it will help the other person think of consequences.

- When the other person speaks very emotionally about a problem, just listen. She doesn't necessarily want a solution. She wants to make this problem sound real to you—that it is not all in her head. Pay attention. Don't internalize the negativity and absorb it or plan what you will say next. Use this as an opportunity to figure out what is bothering the person, deep inside. This is valuable information.

- When you disagree, talk in parts: "A part of me feels sad [scared, angry] . . ." This way you make the other person feel secure that the rest of you likes and values him. You have to explain to your opponent how you feel when you are hurt. He needs to feel empathy for you, or he will do it again.

- If you are asked to do something you don't feel like doing right now—for example, if you are watching a great movie on TV or finishing up a project at work—tell the person that you will take care of it later. Be sure to do it! This is like establishing a good credit rating for future purchases. Make sure you keep your word even for the smallest promise—if you want reciprocity.

- Take the "Why?" out of your questions, which makes another person feel like an accused criminal on the witness stand. For example, instead of asking, "Why didn't you call me the whole day?" state the facts: "I was worried when you didn't call me the whole day."

- Take the intensifiers—adverbs, adjectives, and other hyperbole—out of your speech, which upset other people and yourself by creating drama. Stick to the simple sentence structure of subject, verb, and object without all the embellishments.

- Tone down the rising emotional pitch of your voice, which can cause the other person to feel threatened and shift to the defensive.

- Maintain your posture: shoulders back and down, standing straight with your chest open. This stance means you have a strong position but are open to alternatives (contrast this to standing with arms folded across your chest).

Avoid the Tennis Ball Effect

Overall, during an argument, avoid the tennis ball effect: your opponent hits the ball to you, and you hit the ball back at her. Some rallies last a long time because both players know where the ball is going to land, and no one wants to lose that point. You try to wear each other out. When you fall into an old pattern and expect a different result, you are setting yourself up for failure. Anyone who has ever argued with a teenager has experienced this frustrating pattern. Instead, try hitting the ball from a different angle or wait and see where on the court your opponent is running, then simply hit the ball in the other direction. In the case of that teenager this might mean using a bit of reverse psychology to achieve the result you truly want. What has changed in your normal game plan? You have paused for a moment to view the court through your opponent's eyes. You won the point

TALES OF STRESS ADDICTION
Almost Never on Sunday

My friend Roberta told me about her boss, Ahmad. Ahmad arrived at work early, left late, and came in every Sunday to make sure everything in the computer systems was up and running. His hard work paid off, and he was promoted to managing director. He called a meeting informing the staff to report to work on Sundays. Roberta, high up the ladder herself, spoke up to say that working Sundays would ruin family day; besides, there really wasn't much work to do on the weekend. In fact, she went on, most people would prefer to stay an hour later during the week than come in on Sunday. Ahmad claimed that the system could not be left alone for the whole weekend and that Saturday was his errand and laundry day.

Begrudgingly, everyone submitted to Ahmad's demands except for Roberta. On Sundays, people just hung around the office socializing with Ahmad. During the week, Roberta began experiencing headaches and insomnia. I helped her reframe the conflict with a compassionate spin. Surely she could empathize with Ahmad, who didn't have a family or close friends. Work gave him a meaningful place to go on Sundays. Roberta began to feel sorry for him. She was blessed with a happy marriage and two adorable boys.

The next day she made peace. "Ahmad, I will come in every other Sunday and stay for half a day to show you good faith. Perhaps you can rotate the department, so people can enjoy a complete weekend off too, since you don't need everyone on board, as far as I can see. If there is a problem with the system, I will even come to work in the middle of the night."

Ahmad smiled. "Thank you, Roberta. I appreciate your compromise. I'll make sure to schedule some family outings like softball games and picnics to generate some team spirit throughout the year. You can help me plan them."

cleverly, easily, and gracefully because you were not locked into your own mind-set. When you are in control of yourself, you gain control of the situation! And remember to be a gracious winner and not rub it in. Opponents respond better to grace and civility.

Born to Be Bad

Until now we have focused on reconciling our external conflicts by taking appropriate measures to ensure a good outcome. It's time to enter the inner sanctum and address your internal conflicts, which hinder you from self-actualization and happiness. Discover your self-reliance by confronting your do-I-dare mind-set. It feels good to be bad once in a while because it liberates you from routine restrictions. Being bad connotes that playful, naughty side of living and the freedom to enjoy an activity you are not particularly good at doing. These two attributes are inter-related in uncovering your hidden assets to live life to the max. Afterwards you might experience a little guilt, but this soon passes, as the fun is always worth it. What's bad might turn out to be really good for you.

Being bad at something usually means that you are trying out something new. Whenever you start learning a new sport, dance, or foreign language, you are going to be clumsy, usually god-awful. Enjoy the awkwardness and don't be afraid of being bad in front of others. Eventually you will learn the skill and become proficient; then it's time to be bad at something else in order to grow. I remember the first time I took a step class. Not only was my timing off, but I went left when everyone else went right. When I got good at it, step became terribly boring. I had to take a new class or else become a robot, which is not the point of a good workout.

However, we don't always become proficient when we learn new skills, or even when we continue with hobbies we enjoy doing. In fact, we could be quite bad at an activity for a long time, but we like it nevertheless. I play piano once in a while. I'm no concert pianist, and a few sour notes won't kill anyone's ears. The point is that when I play, this is the music I'm making to express my feelings. What's wrong with a few discordant notes to make myself and others laugh or to emphasize a discordant note in my life? Music isn't made only for musicians and trained ears. Sometimes my soul needs to hear these bad notes!

Unfortunately, we experiment less as we grow older because we are afraid of acting silly or awful. However, we all started out as primitive, instinctive, emotion-driven toddlers, until adults tamed our wild experimentation, curtailing us with propriety and civility. "What will the neighbors say? Where are your manners?" When we grow older and unhappier, this is the time we need to remind ourselves how natural it felt to be bad. We can take our cue from actors who unleash their wild side in a script, because in essence we write our own daily scripts and act in them too.

Some actors—Jack Nicholson, Ed Norton, and Daniel Day-Lewis, for example—seek out bad-boy roles. They enjoy releasing their bad side, without inhibitions, without fear of social condemnation. In fact, the worse they behave, the more kudos they receive for their acting. I was always a model student in school. However, the best part I ever played in a school play was the wicked witch in *Hansel and Gretel*. I loved my primal scream, dark cape, and black hat. Some of my friends described me as a real natural.

Then consider the joys of being bad at a chore such as cooking, the way I am, a victim of learned helplessness. Never fear; it works for me. Guests don't expect me to do much more than the basics, and they always volunteer to bring potluck. Or, for example, if your husband proves to be inept in the kitchen, an age-old trick, he's hoping he won't be asked to help do the dishes ever again. "Sorry, I broke a few." Hate doing the bills at home? A few bad mistakes, and you won't have to do this task anymore either.

All this adds up to the basic truth that bad and good are often trendy judgments based on what's in vogue. Many of us discover over time that what we thought was bad is actually good for us. For example, whole eggs are a high-quality food that doesn't raise our cholesterol as previously thought; women trying to conceive are advised to eat full-fat ice cream every night. Instead of judging whether something is bad or good for you, consider reframing the question: Do I like this, or don't I like this? Does this make me feel comfortable or not? (This does not mean overriding your intuition, your primal instinct, which warns you of danger.) Feeling uncomfortable, feeling the excitement that precedes taking a leap, when all your senses are on high alert, usually translates as bad. Go for it! It's time to leave your comfort zone.

The last time I was in the nail salon with two close friends, I created quite a ruckus. I couldn't stop laughing loudly and making silly girlish comments, as the three of us shared our fantasies and made fun of each other, as if we were in someone's living room instead of a quiet, refined nail salon. People stared at us, but we didn't care. We were having too good of a time. A woman leaned over to me and said, "Honey, I want whatever you're on. What are you taking?"

"I'm not on anything. I'm just high on life."

■ ■ ■

Read on to the last chapter. You are almost ready to introduce the new, improved you to your family and friends.

A New View of You

At last. No more stress. No more stress addiction.

There's a new, calmer you in town who has fortified her identity, who has become proactive about her health and fitness and is determined to have more fun, who is full of joy and spontaneity.

You are excited about being born again, fresh and vital. There's a brand-new day of fewer duties and more breathing space. You can't wait to share your perceptions, but then there are your spouse, your children, your family, your colleagues and friends who might be wondering if your new, improved version of yourself is genuine and here to stay. Also, they might feel insecure about how the new you will be interacting with the old them.

- Family and friends might feel estranged by your new "soft" power—your style, creativity, priorities, and perceptions are different.

- Your spontaneity, joy, and vitality might make their stress-filled lifestyles more noticeable—especially if you are looking happier and younger. Who will be their partners in crime when complaining about everything in life, kvetching about relationships, and eating fatty junk food?

- Your spouse might be jealous of the attention you are getting from other people. Your new positivism could become a magnet.

- Your family might resent the time you spend enjoying special activities for yourself or preparing healthy foods, especially when they do neither.

Etiquette for Getting Reacquainted

Some people will readily embrace change because they love it and thrive on it. Others will be more resistant. Your family might initially feel awkward about getting things right, and worry about what they have to give up because of the way you have changed. You've been catering to their needs for so long. The best way to introduce the new you and share what you have learned is to anticipate their reactions and prepare for them. It's like introducing a new baby to the family when you can foresee the mixed feelings siblings will have.

- Reassure them you still love them.

- Resist the temptation to shock everyone with huge changes all the time.

- Avoid comparisons.

- Create a safe environment for open expression, allowing them to discuss what's bothering them.

- Give yourself plenty of time for your own metamorphosis. You can float awhile as you evaluate and tweak the changes.

- Distance yourself a bit from those people who sabotage your changes until you feel more secure and habituated. Tap into the "yes" people.

Avoid the Dictator-Doormat Syndrome

Keep in mind that no woman is an island unto herself. You will need to get along and achieve a balance and connectivity with your loved ones and friends. Watch out for the temptation of falling into the dictator-doormat syndrome. You possess the tools, and because you are zealous about all that you have learned, there might be a tendency to start correcting everyone around you and preaching to them—in a good way, you think—to enthusiastically share and process the information.

This disposition will not endear you to others. Most people won't get inspired by condescending lectures about the joys of transformation. What a bore. How pretentious. And, ironically, if you try to change them, you'll be reversing in your own journey of self-improvement. You'll be shifting the focus from you to them, all over again. To introduce your new self and share what you learn with others, just be yourself.

At this point in your transformative journey, you've realized the basic paradox that you can change only after you have accepted yourself as you are. Extend that same courtesy to your inner circle. If you want all the significant people in your life to grow, you have to accept them too. When you focus on their strengths, they will mirror themselves in you and keep developing their abilities. They will fulfill your positive prophetic description of them because above all, they want to stay connected to you. Inspire them! Stimulate, but don't annihilate!

You Can Improve Your Marriage

Your transformation can positively affect your spouse, who might fear your change the most, and bring you closer than ever. For example, when you dated your spouse, you made him feel important. He shared his big dreams with you. However, during your marriage, your own self-doubts and symptoms of distress may have led to your disliking yourself. Consciously or unconsciously, you may have transmitted this unhappiness to him. Maybe he couldn't grow in an anxious environment, fraught with the tension of your questioning the meaning of your individual life. Maybe he thinks you're questioning your life with him. When you embrace and respect yourself, you are ready to help him feel more comfortable about himself, as if he possessed a magic talisman that would help him achieve anything he wanted to accomplish.

"What would you do if you knew that you couldn't fail?" you might say. "Well . . . you can't! Not with me. You have my unconditional love."

You can be a source of light to him, a positive coach who uplifts him to accomplish the improbable. The two of you can be a dynamic team. This good energy flows from you to him and back to you, rippling out to the rest of the family and to your friends.

When you have his attention, don't waste it with judgment. It's important to be positive and supportive, because a man desires to maintain his status. If you want openness in your relationship, make him feel that he is indispensable. The environment you create at home should be demilitarized and without disparagement. If he can't feel safe at home, where else can he? Now that you've set the stage for him to talk, let him talk, which means don't interrupt or ask questions too soon—even if he goes into a long monologue. Wait for him to pause or to ask you for your input. This approach sets the stage for him to open up to you, which is what you have wanted all along.

The Difference Between Force and Power

Basically, getting along with all the people in your life means that you have to differentiate between force and power. Trying to force control or dictate The Word to your loved ones is ego driven, and signals that you haven't tapped into your real power yet, that you don't really know how to influence them—yet. Your expanding sphere of influence lies in your ability to connect with others, to tune into them and create harmony, not to compel them. However, connecting with others and showing compassion should not make you last on the list. You must be number one—this is a nonnegotiable. Remember our formula for wellbeing: I do for me = I do for us. Only when you are in harmony with yourself do you create harmony with others.

To feel positive and resilient, we all need to exercise true power, the power of choice, in everything we do. However, remember where your power ends. You are not responsible for anyone's happiness except your own—what a relief not to have to be the rescuer or the martyr! This leaves you with extra time and space.

By now you have gained the power to say no to activities that deplete you. But can you accept a no from others? Self-discovery tempts some of us toward self-congratulation instead of humility, compassion, and understanding the need to build a strong team. Because we've cultivated a strong sense of self throughout this book, the temptation can sometimes be to build a wall around our improved identity to keep it safe and intact. However, this wall could separate you from those you love and restrict your marvelous explorations, limiting your experiences for potential new growth.

This is what I do instead. I have an imaginary remote control with a sensor that raises my wall to protect me when any energy vampires are present and lowers my wall to interact with the people I love and trust. To get a reality check and venture out from my narrow context, however, I regularly admit people who don't agree with me. I rely on my intuition to let me know if they're coming from a place of truth or from their own stressful issues. Self-improvement is not about competing for control, but rather pooling your best resources together—those of your spouse, children, colleagues, or mother-in-law.

Stress Surges

In this book, you've learned that you can't make your personal happiness conditional on someone else's behavior. There will always be something someone says or does that bothers you and has the potential to bring back stress. Make up your mind to appreciate what you have inside yourself and to experience inner peace. Never let little stressors accumulate, as it is much harder

Tips for Curing Stress Addiction
Patience Is a Virtue in Managing Stress

I was chatting with a woman waiting on line at the supermarket. She frowned, "I have a million things to do, and this line is taking forever." The cashier shouted, "Price check—I need a price check!" The woman exploded, "Why do I always pick the wrong line?" I think she wanted to choke me when I blurted out, "The universe is trying to teach you patience." The woman in back of her chimed in, "Yeah, that's what I need more of—patience. I'm always so impatient with everything in my life. I wish I could be patient right now!" I turned to her and said, "Well, you have to be patient about becoming patient." She laughed, "You're right. That's pretty funny."

Patience can make the difference between an inflammatory response, which harms your body and enrages your mind, and a relaxation response, which stabilizes your glucose levels, blood pressure, and digestion and keeps your immune system humming. Patience feels like a deep inhalation of fresh air followed by a deep exhalation of staleness. You feel lighter and receptive to changes that unexpectedly come your way, instead of tapping your foot and rolling your eyes.

Time is subjective, dependent on your perception. When you are having fun, time flies. When you are suffering, impatient with pain or grief, time lasts forever. You can learn patience by observing nature. Look how long it takes a seedling to grow, flower, and bear fruit. Why should you be unnaturally different?

to shed a big stressor when you are descending into depression. You now know all the basic techniques to decompress quickly.

A simple rhythmic action, such as conscious breathing or clenching and unclenching your fists, will help release stress. Eating a complex carbohydrate for a quick pick-me-up, listening to upbeat music, taking a whiff of lavender, and enjoying a few minutes of sunlight will restore enough positive energy to allow you to reframe the negative thought. And, of course, activity alleviates anxiety; it's a naturally potent antidepressant.

These are the relaxation response cues you cultivate during the good times in order to activate the response during the stressful times. You can have fun experimenting with selecting fragrances, snacks, inspirational quotes, visual cues, exercise equipment, and sound therapy. They can come together to create synergy; these are your "well-being tools," ready when you need them most. Because one size does not fit all, it is a good idea to find out ahead of time what works for you.

What Will I Do Differently This Time?

Approximately seven years ago, during a spring workshop when the blossoms were being released from the trees, I turned to my class and said, "I'm going to conduct an experiment. Since my teenage years I have suffered from sinus headaches from May through October depending on the allergens in the air and, of course, the changes in barometric pressure. I could predict a storm with great accuracy. Today I am throwing my Allegra D in the garbage. Instead, I am going to take my own advice and keep myself in balance, body and mind: eating right, exercising, expressing myself, having fun, and carving out quiet time for me. By managing the little stressors, I will let my immune system deal with the big stressor, inflammation. I shouldn't need any medication for my sinus headaches. I will breathe deeply, inhaling and exhaling, slowing down and resting whenever I feel a headache coming on. I'm going to add more fiber to my diet and drink more water to flush out toxins."

Most of my class was skeptical about this mind-over-matter approach, predicting I would be back on the medication soon. I have not taken any allergy medication since that day and have had no more allergy headaches.

The first two weeks were the hardest, as I was breaking an addiction to the pain-relief medication. However, core training exercises to get the blood pumping into my head, balanced with quiet time, made all the difference. True, I might have been a little short fused during that time, but I alerted my family so that they would understand that it was me and not them.

Because throwing away my allergy medication was my choice and under my control, I was well prepared to deal with the ensuing stress response. However, there will be times when you experience a stress surge—when financial responsibilities pile up, unexpected family conflicts arise, or critical changes take place in your body. Many of these stressors will be out of your control. Your stress levels could approach the danger zone. How do you keep from exploding, as if triggering an old reflex?

The key is to plan ahead for the stressful times and practice what you have learned. Conjure up typical recurring stressful situations in your mind, the more disturbing the better. Then mentally script them with a calmer, honest dialogue to take out the sting. Rehearse and revise the dialogue before the negative situation occurs. This practice will provide you with the "experience" that will help you redefine new problems and improve your resiliency to obstacles, ultimately placing you in command of the situation as a self-assured woman.

This is your opportunity to address all those "Should have, could have, would have said" statements you are so adept at making after the fact. Ask yourself, What will I do differently this time? Rehearse them in your mind the way athletes visualize success before a competition. Should one of these scenarios occur in real life, you will possess the imaginative experience to quickly decompress and respond rationally—the way you always wanted to do before stress jumbled the words.

For example, my husband, Steve, is chronically late, whereas I pride myself on the integrity of honoring time and place. On the rare occasion that Steve can possibly be on time, he will look for something to do at the last minute to ensure that he'll be late. The more I would say, "Hurry up. We'll be late," the worse it became. The car ride was usually hellish. On two separate occasions, out of haste Steve hit a pothole and tore a tire. I decided to change my tactics. Steve was running late, but I said nothing. My silence caused him to wonder what I was plotting, which was absolutely nothing. During the mad car ride I made small talk and turned on the radio. Steve asked me if I was annoyed at him for our being late.

"Not at all. I have accepted being late as a given, and we'll get there when we get there. You have other redeeming qualities."

The next time we had a social engagement or a performance, Steve was on time—ready before I was.

"What's taking you so long? We'll be late."

When you stop pushing so hard, the other person stops pulling away.

What Am I Not Seeing About the Other Side?

Since you have discovered your individual "I," you have been focusing inward on *your* passion print, *your* fulfillment, *your* transformation, and *your* happiness. This process has helped you emerge into the light of creativity and self-empowerment to advocate for yourself.

I've always been fascinated by the idea that "I" and "eye" are homonyms: an I for an eye, so to speak. The eye (I) that has turned inward has helped you gain greater *insight* about yourself. Now it's time to look outward with your other eye and see your family, friends, and colleagues, too. You have two eyes: I + I to see the whole big picture. Keep in mind the following questions:

- What is important to your family?

- What are their vulnerabilities?

- Do you goad any of the people in your life into fulfilling a negative prophecy?

When you have a strong sense of self, you don't need to jump to conclusions because of personal insecurity, fear, or doubt. You can discern people's motivation and actions with a wide-angle peripheral view. Doing so will help you tolerate some of their aggravating quirks, which might in fact be their attempts to be helpful. Most of the difficult situations you will need to reframe and let go of are related to the things you allowed to be done to you because you never spoke up about all that you were compelled to do. Now that you are a healthy narcissist, you can say no, delegate chores to others, and let some duties fall by the wayside. Proper self-care—eating right, exercising, and getting sufficient sleep—help you to consistently see the middle ground through the eyes of a realistic optimist.

If the new you feels that you are regressing to old, irritable knee-jerk reactions, think about the probable stressful trigger so as to objectify it with awareness.

- I am tired.

- I am being a worrier—call me Chicken Little.

- I misunderstood.

- Others are abrupt because of their own stressors.

- Others want to help out, but not according to my rigid time frame.

- There is an underlying reason why they can't do it; something affected them while they were growing up.

- I'm asking people to be perfectionists and achieve the unattainable. This makes them feel like failures.

- I'm asking people to change their nature. They're not me.

- I set too high expectations for others, and as a result they disappoint me.

The Recognizable Signs of Having Achieved a Good Self-Concept

In Step 2 you took a quiz to help you tap into your submerged identity, and in another questionnaire you rated your self-esteem. Having completed this book, you will find it helpful to gauge your self-growth, to understand where you still need to go, by answering the following questions:

1. Do you express your opinions without fear, because you are confident and honest? ___ Yes ___ No

2. Do you trust your intuition and not override your instincts when making important choices? ___ Yes ___ No

3. Do you visualize like a champion what you want to have in life, in order to manifest your destiny? In other words, do you conceive, believe, achieve? ___ Yes ___ No

4. Do you tap into your creative energy, especially when destructive things happen in your life, enabling you to revitalize? ___ Yes ___ No

5. Does change feel natural and necessary for growth and self-improvement? ___ Yes ___ No

6. Do you let go of the need to be right all the time and respect other people's belief systems? ___ Yes ___ No

7. Do you question your own tribal beliefs when they are not working for you? ___ Yes ___ No

8. Can you go an entire day without wearing your wristwatch during vacation? ___ Yes ___ No

9. Do you stay focused on whatever you are doing in the present? ___ Yes ___ No

10. Do you dress to suit yourself—mix and match clothes that express who you are today? ___ Yes ___ No

11. Do you have an accessory that expresses who you are, one that people can identify with you, such as a fragrance or a simple necklace that you always wear? ___ Yes ___ No

12. Do you check yourself in the mirror and say, "Hey, good looking"? ___ Yes ___ No

13. Do you see the middle ground? ___ Yes ___ No

14. Do you feel that life does not always have to be comfortable? ___ Yes ___ No

15. Do you feel lucky? ___ Yes ___ No

If you answered yes to just six questions, you are well on your way to reclaiming your joy and spontaneity. You know who you are and where you are going. You will get there. Strengthen your body with healthy eating and exercise to support you on your path to your next happiness: achieve stability before mobility.

You now stand at the top landing of these seven steps, able to see from a higher vantage point, the entire panorama. You have all the seeds you need for happiness. It's your time to bloom.

Keep in mind that the path inward is never straight. Human beings are bundles of marvelous contradictions. You can champion the green movement, yet sometimes you do not recycle a plastic bag. You can adhere to a healthy meal plan, yet once in a while indulge in a decadent molten chocolate dessert. You will escape for an exciting adventure provided you can return safely home.

I urge you to leave the straight lines of your personality from time to time, taking a few detours along the way to liberate your hidden girl with joy, spontaneity, fun, good humor, and novelty. She will tease you out of your shell as she dances, tambourine in hand, leading you on the lifelong journey to embrace yourself.

If you have needed accomplishment after accomplishment to validate your self-worth, yet have never felt quite satisfied and at peace, revel in solitude as an opportunity to reconnect with your hidden girl. She is waiting patiently for you. Keep yourself aligned with her, because she is your best friend. Feel your body and listen to the song in your heart. She will remind you if you have forgotten the words.

Smile deeply within.

NOTES

Step One

2   *Two studies from Princeton University and the University of Penn-sylvania:* Krueger, Alan B. "Are We Having More Fun Yet? Categorizing and Evaluation Changes in Time Allocation." Unpublished manuscript, Princeton University, Aug. 2005; Stevenson, Betsey, and Justin Wolfers. "The Paradox of Declining Female Happiness." Unpublished manuscript, University of Pennsylvania, Sept. 16, 2007; Leonhardt, David. "He's Happier, She's Less So." *New York Times.* Sept. 26, 2007. www.nytimes.com/2007 /09/26/business/26leonhardt.html?ref=business.

3   *And further research from Sigal Barsade:* Barsade, Sigal G., and Donald E Gibson. "Why Does Affect Matter in Organizations?" *Academy of Management Perspectives,* Feb. 2007, pp. 36–59.

19 *Did you know that in married working couples:* Gupta, Sanjiv. "Autonomy, Dependence, or Display? The Relationship Between Married Women's Earnings and Housework." *Journal of Marriage and the Family,* 2007, 69(2), 399–417.

23 *It's well known that exposure to viruses:* University of Saskatchewan. "VIDO Finds New Link Between Stress and Disease Susceptibility." *Omics: A Journal of Integrative Biology,* Dec. 20, 2007. www.usask.ca/research/news/read.php?id=763.

25 *The latest research from Harvard:* Christakis, Nicholas A., and Paul Allison. "Mortality After Hospitalization of a Spouse." *New England Journal of Medicine,* Feb. 16, 2006, 354, 719–730.

37   *According to the American Medical Association:* Miller, Michael
Craig. "Type D Personality Traits Can Hurt Heart Health."
Harvard Mental Health Letter, Nov. 2007. www.health.harvard
.edu/press_releases/type_d_personality.htm

Step Two

45   *Women who suppress their thoughts and feelings:* Eacker, Elaine,
and others. "Marital Status, Marital Strain, and Risk of
Coronary Heart Disease or Total Mortality: The Framingham
Offspring Study." *Psychosomatic Medicine,* July-Aug. 2007, 69,
509–513.

Step Four

90   *Women ages forty to sixty involved in a study:* Simon, Gregory.
"Association Between Obesity and Depression in Middle-Aged
Women." *General Hospital Psychiatry,* Jan. 2008, 30, 32–39.

92   *Sleep deprivation threatens:* Colten, Harvey. "U.S. Lacks Ade-
quate Capacity to Treat People with Sleep Disorders." Institute
of Medicine, Apr. 2006. www8.nationalacademies.org/onpinews
/newsitem.aspx?RecordID=11617.

97   *To keep your mood up:* Kleiner, Susan, and Bob Condor. *The
Good Mood Diet.* New York: Springboard Press, 2007.

99   *And don't ignore the power of touch:* Coan, James, and others.
"Lending a Hand: Social Regulation of the Neural Response
to Threat." *Psychological Science,* Dec. 2006, 17, 1032–1039.

101   *Did you know that the order:* Wurtman, Judith, and Margaret
Danbrot. *Managing Your Mind and Mood Through Food.* New
York: Rawson Associates, 1986.

105   *When you are in a negative frame of mind:* Hirsch, Alan.
Life's a Smelling Success. Shasta, Calif.: Authors of Unity,
2003.

105   *Duke University's Marian Butterfeld:* Laino, Charles. "Smell of
Grapefruit Helps Women Look Younger." WebMD.
www.webmd.com/content/Article/106/108196.htm.

106   *One extensive Finnish study concludes:* Hu, Gang, and others. "The Effects of Physical Activity and Body Mass Index on Cardiovascular, Cancer and All-Cause Mortality Among 47,212 Middle-Aged Finnish Men and Women." *International Journal of Obesity*, Aug. 2005, *29*, 894–902.

107   *An Italian study shows:* "Walking and Moderate Exercise Help Prevent Dementia." Dec. 19, 2007. American Academy of Neurology. www.aan.com/press/index.cfm?fuseaction=release .view&release=568.

107   *According to the American Psychological Association:* "Exercise Fuels the Brain's Stress Buffers." American Psychological Association Help Center. www.apahelpcenter.org/articles /article.php?id=25.

113   *Neuroscientist Fred Gage from Columbia University explains:* Gage, Fred. "Lobes of Steel." *New York Times*, Aug. 19, 2005. www .nytimes.com/2007/08/19/sports/playmagazine/0819play-brain .html?_r=1&pagewanted=2&ei=5087&em&en=29f32f97d776f 635&ex=1187841600&oref=slogin.

113   *University of Illinois scientists studied school-age children:* Gage, 2005.

Step Five

125   *The American Medical Association has officially labeled:* Robinson, Bryan E. *Chained to the Desk*. New York: New York University Press, 2001.

127   *One study found that when the human:* Allen, Karen, and others. "Cardiovascular Reactivity and the Presence of Pets, Friends, and Spouses: The Truth About Cats and Dogs." *Psychosomatic Medicine*, 2002, *64*, 727–739.

131   *People who kid around with their spouses:* Gottman, John, and Nan Silver. *The Seven Principles for Making a Marriage Work*. New York: Three Rivers Press, 1999.

132   *Studies reviewed by Robert Provine:* Provine, Robert. *Laughter: A Scientific Investigation*. New York: Penguin, 2001.

132 *Researchers at Stanford University reported:* Stanford University
School of Medicine. "Gender Differences Are a Laughing
Matter, Stanford Brain Study Shows." Nov. 5, 2005. http://med
.stanford.edu/news_releases/2005/november/humor.html.

133 *A woman who deploys a typically male sense of humor:* Lawson,
Willow. "Humor's Sexual Side." *Psychology Today*, Sept.-Oct.
2005. http://psychologytoday.com/articles/index.php?term
=20050808-000003&page=1.

Step Six

150 *Sure, anthropologist Helen Fisher . . . claims:* Fisher, Helen. *Why
We Love: The Nature and Chemistry of Romantic Love.* New York:
Henry Holt, 2004.

150 *In one study, 30 percent of couples admitted:* Gilbert, Susan.
"Married with Problems? Therapy May Not Help. *New York
Times*, Apr. 19, 2005. www.nytimes.com/2005/04/19/health
/psychology/19coup.html.

150 *The latest neuroscientific research has sifted:* Kluger, Jeffrey.
"Why We Love." *Time*, Jan. 28, 2008, pp. 55–60.

151 *The non-divorced but wed-locked syndrome:* Rozhon, Tracie.
"New Homes, Separate His-and-Her Bedrooms." *New York
Times*, Mar. 11, 2007. www.nytimes.com/2007/03/11/us
/11separate.html?pagewanted=2&_r=1.

152 *Psychologist Gordon Gallup . . . explains:* Kluger, 2008.

160 *Repetitive, purposeless arguing is a big turnoff:* Gottman, John,
and Nan Silver. *The Seven Principles for Making a Marriage Work.*
New York: Three Rivers Press, 1999.

161 *A good fight with your spouse:* Harburg, Ernest. "Marital Pair
Anger-Coping Types May Act as an Entity to Affect Mortality."
Journal of Family Communication, Jan. 2008, 8, 44–61.

162 *Physicians like Mehmet Oz recommend:* Roizen, Michael, F., and
Mehmet C. Oz. "Love Can Benefit Your Health as Well as Any
Drug: Let Us Count the Ways." *Reader's Digest*, Feb. 2006.

www.rd.com/columnists/oz-and-roizen/health-benefits-of-love-and-sex/article.html.

169 *John Renner, founder of the Consumer Health Information Research Institute:* Nordenberg, Tamar. "Looking for a Libido Lift? The Facts About Aphrodisiacs." *FDA Consumer Magazine*, Feb. 1996. www.fda.gov/fdac/features/196_love.html.

169 *Italian researchers claim:* Salonia, Andrea, and others. "Chocolate and Women's Sexual Health: An Intriguing Correlation." *Journal of Sexual Medicine*, May 2006, pp. 476–482.

169 *Scientists advise . . . the so-called Mediterranean diet:* Pizzorno, Joseph. "Better Sex, Mediterranean-Style." WebMD. Sept. 4, 2007. http://blogs.webmd.com/integrative-medicine-wellness/2007/09/better-sex-mediterranean-style.html.

173 *As of 2001, fourteen million prescriptions of Viagra:* Wysoski, Diane K., and Joslyn Swann. "Use of Medications for Erectile Dysfunction in the United States 1996 Through 2001." *Journal of Urology*, Mar. 2003, 163(3), 1040–1042.

Step Seven

178 *There's more road rage than ever before:* Duggan, Paul. "Death Reflects Area's Unabated Road Rage." *Washington Post*, Oct. 24, 2005, p. B1.

179 *According to Martin Seligman:* Seligman, Martin. *Authentic Happiness.* New York: Simon & Schuster, 2002.

188 *For example, I asked Edwene Gaines:* From an interview with Edwene Gaines on my radio show, *Turn On Your Inner Light,* Dec. 13, 2005. Posted on my site: www.turnonyourinnerlight.com/page3.html.

191 *That's just how it is, for people make snap judgments:* Gladwell, Malcolm. *Blink: The Power of Thinking Without Thinking.* New York: Little, Brown, 2005.

RESOURCES

For the most current information on stress addiction and to contact me, visit my Web site: www.addictedtostress.com, which is updated regularly.

For the Body

To learn science-based information about how to improve your health and that of your family and to read suggestions of tasty ways to incorporate more servings of fruits and vegetables into your diet, visit www.5aday.org.

To find out the latest fitness trends along with exercises for all ages, visit the all-in-one site for fitness and healthy eating from the notable experts: www.fitnessonline.com.

To learn about massage therapy and what's involved in selecting a qualified masseuse, visit the Web site of the American Massage Therapy Association: www.amtamassage.org.

For deep breathing and biofeedback to generate better health by lowering stress levels, see Andrew Weil's *Breathing: The Master Key to Healing,* and his CD set on mindfulness meditation, *Meditation for Optimum Health,* copresented with Jon Kabat-Zinn.

For the Mind

To learn how to be in the moment, see www.mindfulnesstapes .com, featuring Jon Kabat-Zinn, a stress-reduction expert in mindfulness meditation for everyday living.

To learn how to relax and even to get rid of headaches, visit this great interactive Web site with Belleruth Naperstek: www.healthjourneys.com.

To lower your anxiety and get hypnotic help with your diet, visit Dr. Steven Gurgevich's site: www.tranceformation.com.

To restore your relationship with your spouse and children, visit the Gottman Institute: www.gottman.com; phone: (888) 523-9042 or (206) 523-9042.

To learn more about nonviolent communication, which uses empathy as its basic training technique, visit: the Center for Nonviolent Communication: www.cnvc.org; phone: (903) 893-3886.

For Further Reading

Ariely, Dan. *Predictably Irrational*. New York: HarperCollins, 2008.

Atkins, Dale. *I'm Okay, You're My Parents*. New York: Henry Holt, 2004.

Beck, Judith. *The Beck Diet Solution Weight Loss Workbook*. Birmingham, Ala.: Oxmoor House, 2007.

Brantley, Jeff, and Wendy Millstine. *Five Good Minutes at Work*. Oakland, Calif.: New Harbinger, 2007.

Clarke, David. *They Can't Find Anything Wrong*. Boulder, Colo.: Sentient, 2007.

Cutler, Ellen W., and Jeremy E. Kaslow. *Micro Miracles*. Emmaus, Penn.: Rodale, 2005.

DeBroff, Stacy. *The Mom Book Goes to School*. New York: Free Press, 2005.

Fowers, Blaine J. *Beyond the Myth of Marital Happiness: How Embracing the Virtues of Loyalty, Generosity, Justice, and Courage Can Strengthen Your Relationship*. San Francisco: Jossey-Bass, 2000.

Gurgevich, Steven, and Joy Gurgevich. *The Self-Hypnosis Diet*. Boulder, Colo.: Sounds True, 2007.

Haltzman, Scott, and Teresa Foy diGeronimo. *The Secrets of Happily Married Men*. San Francisco: Jossey-Bass, 2006.

Haltzman, Scott, and Teresa Foy diGeronimo. *The Secrets of Happily Married Women*. San Francisco: Jossey-Bass, 2008.

Hirsch, Alan. *Life's a Smelling Success*. Shasta, Calif.: Authors of Unity, 2003.

Hurst, Andrea, and Beth Wilson. *The Lazy Dog's Guide to Enlightenment*. Novato, Calif.: New World Library, 2007.

Liponis, Mark. *UltraLongevity*. New York: Little, Brown, 2007.

Markman, Howard, Scott Stanley, and Susan L. Blumberg. *Fighting for Your Marriage*. (Rev. ed.) San Francisco: Jossey-Bass, 2001.

McCredie, Scott. *Balance*. New York: Little, Brown, 2007.

Page, Susan. *Why Talking Is Not Enough*. San Francisco: Jossey-Bass, 2006.

Peeke, Pamela. *Body for Life for Women*. Emmaus, Penn.: Rodale, 2005.

Ratey, John J. *Spark*. New York: Little, Brown, 2008.

Siegel, Bernie S. *101 Exercises for the Soul*. Novato, Calif.: New World Library, 2005.

Welshons, John E. *When Prayers Aren't Answered*. Novato, Calif.: New World Library, 2007.

ABOUT THE
AUTHOR

Debbie Mandel, MA, is a stress management specialist, radio show host, mind-body lecturer, creator of an educational Web site (www.addictedtostress.com), and the author of two self-help books: *Turn On Your Inner Light: Fitness for Body, Mind and Soul* and *Changing Habits: The Caregivers' Total Workout*.

Debbie conducts stress management workshops for couples, medical personnel, cancer survivors, caregivers, nuns, teachers, young mothers, children, and others. In addition to appearing as a guest on numerous radio shows nationwide, she hosts her own health and fitness radio show on WGBB in New York (which airs Tuesdays from 7:00 PM to 7:30 PM and streams live on the Internet; all shows are archived on her Web site (www.addictedto stress.com).

She has been written about or significantly quoted in such magazines as *Glamour, Oxygen, Cosmopolitan,* and *Woman's World* and in such newspapers as the *New York Times,* the *New York Post,* the *Los Angeles Times,* and the *London Times.* She has been interviewed on TV shows nationwide.

Debbie earned a BA from Brooklyn College, graduating Phi Beta Kappa and summa cum laude, and an MA from New York University Graduate School of Arts and Sciences. She was a high school English teacher and a college professor, and has since utilized her educational experience to help you "read life to get a sense of who you are."

She was a caregiver to two parents with Alzheimer's, which helped her gain an ability to be fully present. She embraces life with a sense of humor and fun, which she brings to her own marriage of thirty-six years to her husband, Steven. She is the mother of three children (Michael, thirty-two; David, twenty-seven; and Amanda, eighteen), and her hobbies include gardening and landscaping, exercising, meditation, and belly dancing.

INDEX